T0360503

Manual for Developing Intercultural Competencies

This book presents a structured yet flexible methodology for developing intercultural competence in a variety of contexts, both formal and informal. Piloted around the world by UNESCO, this methodology has proven to be effective in a range of different contexts and focused on a variety of different issues. It, therefore, can be considered an important resource for anyone concerned with effectively managing the growing cultural diversity within our societies to ensure inclusive and sustainable development.

Intercultural competence refers to the skills, attitudes, and behaviors needed to improve interactions across difference, whether within a society (differences due to age, gender, religion, socio-economic status, political affiliation, ethnicity, and so on) or across borders. The book serves as a tool to develop those competences, presenting an innovative adaptation of what could be considered an ancient tradition of storytelling found in many cultures. Through engaging in the methodology, participants develop key elements of intercultural competence, including greater self-awareness, openness, respect, reflexivity, empathy, increased awareness of others, and in the end, greater cultural humility.

This book will be of great interest to intercultural trainers, policy makers, development practitioners, educators, community organizers, civil society leaders, university lecturers, and students – all who are interested in developing intercultural competence as a means to understand and appreciate difference, develop relationships with those across difference, engage in intercultural dialogue, and bridge societal divides.

Darla K. Deardorff is a research scholar at Duke University, author of 8 books and over 50 articles and book chapters, founder of ICC Global and the World Council on Intercultural and Global Competence, affiliated faculty at numerous institutions around the world, and frequently invited speaker and consultant.

Routledge Focus on Environment and Sustainability

For more information about this series, please visit: www.routledge.com/
Routledge-Focus-on-Environment-and-Sustainability/book-series/RFES

Manual for Developing Intercultural Competencies
Story Circles

Darla K. Deardorff

First published 2020
by the United Nations Educational, Scientific and Cultural Organization
(UNESCO), 7, place de Fontenoy, 75352 Paris 07 SP, France

and Routledge
2 Park Square, Milton Park, Abingdon, Oxon OX14 4RN

and by Routledge
52 Vanderbilt Avenue, New York, NY 10017

Routledge is an imprint of the Taylor & Francis Group, an informa business

© 2020 UNESCO

UNESCO ISBN 978-92-3-100331-8

Trademark notice: Product or corporate names may be trademarks
or registered trademarks, and are used only for identification and
explanation without intent to infringe.

British Library Cataloguing-in-Publication Data
A catalogue record for this book is available from the British Library

Library of Congress Cataloging-in-Publication Data
A catalog record for this book has been requested

ISBN: 978-0-367-19997-5 (hbk)
ISBN: 978-0-429-24461-2 (ebk)

Typeset in Times New Roman
by Apex CoVantage, LLC

Contents

Figures/tables/photos/boxes

Figures

Tables

Photos

Boxes

Foreword

All societies in our contemporary world are the result of intercultural communication. They are built on the momentum of cultural diversity, which has been a source of strength and transformation throughout human history. This is particularly clear today, in a world where a great diversity of people live closely together, their co-existence intensified by social media and technological communication, changing the economic and cultural landscapes even in the most remote places.

Although individuals and communities are more connected than ever, conflicts and misunderstandings persist between and within societies. Hate speech spreads the idea that diversity and unity are irreconcilable and fuels violent acts that can dissolve the social fabric in the long term. The world is torn by conflicts and wars, and new global challenges and threats – such as populism, deep inequalities, and violent extremism – are on the rise, undermining women and men's abilities to live together.

UNESCO's mandate is essential to address these pressing challenges, as it aims to build peace in the minds of men and women by building mutual understanding. In this regard, promoting intercultural dialogue is essential, and UNESCO has been appointed as the lead agency in the United Nations System for the International Decade for the Rapprochement of Cultures (2013–2022).

Fostering intercultural dialogue means, above all, to give access to every people's culture and history and highlight the continuous articulations between cultural diversity and universal values to show the ways in which intercultural exchanges fuel humanity's vitality.

This is at stake in UNESCO's role to promote the universal value of the elements of the cultural World Heritage, as in the Constitution of General and Regional Histories showing how our heritage is the result of a history of mutual influences between civilizations.

As opportunities to listen, share, talk, and understand have multiplied, we have a pivotal role in encouraging and fostering these exchanges so that humanity further benefits from such communication. To do this, we need to ensure that every culture has access to the adequate means of communication and information and can make its voice heard.

As intercultural dialogue is above all a dialogue between peoples, its main day-to-day challenges are to change mindsets to foster respect and openness and to provide men and women with the means to engage with each other.

Education is one of our major means to convey these values and to achieve the goals of the 2030 Agenda for Sustainable Development, adopted by the United Nations, to provide individuals with key competencies to act as engaged and responsible citizens in today's world. However, these skills also have to be part of a lifelong process based on experience and reflection, gathering cognitive, affective, and motivational elements. This is the reason for initiatives to empower individuals with the skills to manage personal encounters and experiences with "cultural others" and engage in intercultural dialogue.

It is in this spirit that the *Manual for Developing Intercultural Competencies* proposes the flexible and adaptable tool of Story Circles. Through the technique of storytelling, the manual aims to facilitate positive peace by cultivating intercultural dialogue through the strengthening of interaction and understanding across differences.

Prior to this publication, the methodology of Story Circles was tested by UNESCO in five countries across different regions of the world – with Youth in Thailand and Tunisia, sexual minorities in Zimbabwe, indigenous peoples in Costa Rica, and immigrant pupils in Austria. In all pilots, participants reported that they had acquired strong skills for tolerance, empathy, critical thinking, and *listening for understanding*.

I hope that this manual will be a powerful instrument to scale up cultural literacy and mutual understanding. By giving opportunities to every woman and man to familiarize herself or himself with intercultural competencies, UNESCO is definitely contributing to reinforcing the foundations for lasting and peaceful societies.

Audrey Azoulay
Director-General of UNESCO

Acknowledgements

Following the publication of "Intercultural Competencies: Conceptual and Operational Framework" in 2013, UNESCO created a concrete, adaptable, and effective tool to fill the gap among the existing methodologies in the field of intercultural competencies. To assess the regional applicability of the tool, to train facilitators, and to refine the methodology, pilot sessions were undertaken in Thailand, Zimbabwe, Costa Rica, Austria, and Tunisia. An abbreviated version of the Story Circles methodology was also implemented in Vanuatu.

We would like to thank all the young women and men who took part in these Story Circles pilot exercises, as well as the partners who contributed to its success:

In Bangkok, Thailand – Mr. Ellyas Enda Hadinata Bangun, former Thailand country manager for AIESEC; Mr. Joel Mark Barredo, program manager for research at SHAPE-SEA, Mahidol University; Dr. Pablo Ramirez, Dr. Patama Satawedin, and Dr. Chutima Kessadayurat of Bangkok University; and Ms. Nuanrudee Kaewtha, Ms. Tadtanee Seeopa, and Chanon Buddharaksa from the Asian Maritime Technological College.

In Harare, Zimbabwe – representatives from UNFPA, Katswe Sistahood, Restless Development ZiCHIRe, and Magitare Trust for participating in the Train the Trainers workshop. Special thanks to Restless Development, Magitare Trust, and Katswe Sistahood for support in mobilizing the participants and for facilitating the pilot sessions in the community.

In San José, Costa Rica – Ms. Viviana Boza Chacón, Vice Minister of Youth and the Ministry of Culture and Youth of Costa Rica; the Vice Ministry of the Presidency for Political Affairs and Social Dialogue from Costa Rica; Parque la Libertad; the Office of the Ombudsperson in Costa Rica; and the Spanish Cultural Centre in Costa Rica

(El Farolito). UNESCO also recognizes the valuable contributions of Contra Corriente, Costa Rica Indígena, Coto Brus CISG, Earth University, Iron Kids of the World, Justicia Restaurativa Surgir, Literofilia, and Sembrando Sonrisas.

In Vienna, Austria – Ms. Aloisia Wörgetter, former Head of Unit "Intercultural and Interreligious Dialogue" (now Austrian Ambassador to Belarus) and Mr. Ernst-Peter Brezovszky, Head of UNESCO Unit, both from the Austrian Federal Ministry for Europe, Integration, and Foreign Affairs. The Federal Ministry of Europe, Integration and Foreign Affairs, who coordinated the pilot in Vienna; Ms Iris Rehklau and Ms Mirela Memic from the Austrian Integration Fund, who participated in the Training of Trainers session and facilitated the sessions with schoolchildren in the Franz-Jonas-Europaschule. Special thanks also go to the director of the school, Mr. Christian Klar, for his hospitality and openness to letting the schoolchildren participate in a Story Circle experience. Our sincere gratitude goes to Claudia Reinpreicht, ambassador at the Austrian delegation to UNESCO, who orchestrated the entire endeavor, and to Ms. Katharina Schaufler, who facilitated the joint efforts between Vienna and Paris.

In Tunis, Tunisia – our gratitude goes to the officials from the Arab Institute of Human Rights, in particular President Abdelbasset Ben Hassen, Director Lamia Grar, Mr. Wahid Chehed, Ms. Nada Ben Faiza, Ms. Hela Cherif, and Mr. Aziz Belatek.

Special recognition goes to the colleagues from UNESCO's field offices (Bangkok, Harare, San José, Rabat, and Apia) who assisted in the organization of all pilots.

We would also like to thank Mr. Abe Radkin, Executive Director of the Aladdin Project, for having integrated the Manual for Developing Intercultural Competencies as a permanent feature in the International Summer University for Intercultural Leadership (IUIL), held each year in Istanbul, Turkey.

We are particularly grateful to those who contributed with texts to this publication, thus reporting their personal experience with the Story Circles methodology: Mr. Adam Sharpe, Mr. Farai Muronzi, Ms. Luciana Batalla Bunn, Ms. Maria del Mar Obando Boza, Ms. Iris Rehklau, Ms. Anna Haase, Mr. Kheireddini Abdelli, Ms. Yasmine Wartani, Mr. Sacha Silbermann Apeloig, and Mr. Harry James Olikwailafa. Our heartfelt thanks go to the young student Ms. Islem Briki for the permission to publish her poem.

The final manuscript was peer-reviewed by Mr. Dov Lynch and Mr. Hugue Ngandeu Ngatta, who provided constructive comments and suggestions. This manual would not have been possible without the firm support of Ms. Nada Al-Nashif, the UNESCO Assistant Director-General for Social and Human Sciences.

The author of the manual, Professor Darla K. Deardorff, wishes to express her gratitude to the experts and students around the world who participated in the interviews, focus groups, and reviews of this methodology and manual, in particular: Dr. Lily Arasaratnam-Smith, Dr. Mattia Baiutti, Dr. Ina Baumann, Dr. John Biewen, Ms. Dana Cassell, Dr. Duane Deardorff, Dr. Makiko Deguchi, Dr. Prue Holmes, Dr. Catherine Jaeger, Dr. Sonja Knutson, Ms. Kathryn Rosenbaum, Mr. Craig Storti, and Dr. Yian Wang, as well as students at Duke University (US), National University of Singapore (Singapore), Nelson Mandela University (South Africa), North Carolina State University (US), Shanghai International Studies University (China), Thammasat University (Thailand), Toyo University (Japan), and Universidad de los Andes (Colombia), as well as participants in the Summer Institute for Intercultural Communication in the US, BCCIE Conference in Canada, NAFSA Conference in the US, BFSU Beijing Teachers Conference in China, Harvard University Global Education Think Tank in the US, REIES Conference in Ecuador, and the amazing UNESCO team in Paris. Professor Deardorff wants to acknowledge the work of civil rights activist Mr. John O'Neal and of Ms. Kay Pranis, whose work on circle processes helped to provide a foundation for this methodology, as well as the much earlier work of Ms. Rachel Davis DuBois, which served as an inspiration for developing this methodology further.

UNESCO and the author also wish to acknowledge that circle processes as such are rooted in traditions and ways of life of indigenous communities, and express appreciation to the indigenous leaders who shared their circle processes with non-native peoples in the 1970s as a way of bringing people together to resolve differences and conflicts.

UNESCO Editorial Team

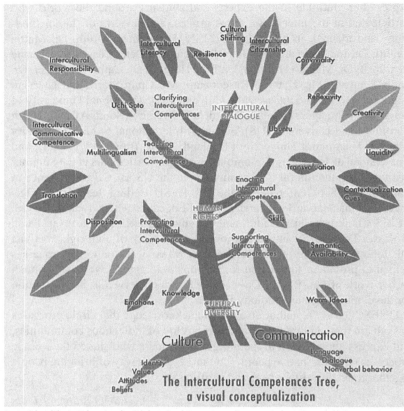

The Intercultural Competences Tree,
a visual conceptualization

Roots: Culture (Identity, Values, Attitudes, Beliefs, etc.) and Communication (Language, Dialogue, Nonverbal behavior, etc.)
Trunk: Cultural Diversity, Human Rights, Intercultural Dialogue
Branches: Operational steps (Clarifying, Teaching, Promoting, Supporting and Enacting Intercultural Competences)
Leaves: Intercultural Responsibility, Intercultural Literacy, Resilience, Cultural Shifting, Intercultural Citizenship, Conviviality, Reflexivity, Creativity, Liquidity, Contextualization Cues, Transvaluation, Ubuntu, Semantic Availability, Warm Ideas, Skills, Uchi Soto, Multilingualism, Disposition, Emotions, Knowledge, Translation, Intercultural Communicative Competence. Some of the leaves have been left free so that this tree, which is very much alive, can be complemented upon the rich diversity of contexts available worldwide.

Figure 0.1 UNESCO Intercultural Competencies Tree

This UNESCO Intercultural Tree provides a map for understanding the different dimensions involved in intercultural relations.

Source: **UNESCO. (2013b).** *Intercultural Competencies: Conceptual and Operational Framework*. Paris: UNESCO

1 Background

Introduction

"The costs of intercultural incompetence are so high, including all the dangers of conflict and war . . . just as our future depends upon actions taken today, so the future of cultural diversity respectful of human rights in our social world depends upon our ability to gain and demonstrate intercultural competencies today" (UNESCO, 2013b, p. 38). Given the grave global challenges facing humans in the 21st century, learning how to live together becomes an imperative. The growth of violent extremism, the mounting migration and displacement crises, and the rise of divisive political populism have underscored the need of expanding, consolidating, and intensifying dialogue among peoples with different cultural backgrounds and beliefs, contributing thus to counter hate speeches and to foster a culture of peace.

What does it take to live together peacefully? How can we bridge societal divides that only seem to be increasing? How can we understand others better, especially those whose beliefs and practices may be quite different? And what can be done to help intentionally enhance others' ability to live and work together across differences that seem to separate, and at times engulf, humans leading to conflict and even war? These questions are addressed through the work of the United Nations Educational, Scientific and Cultural Organization (UNESCO) and other organizations through such terms as intercultural competencies and intercultural dialogue. Much of the work done around these ideas still lacks the specifics of what this means for individuals (and organizations working to enhance individuals' intercultural competencies). This manual attempts to address this void by addressing the individual level and, in so doing, provide a very practical way for anyone to work toward developing intercultural competencies, which is so desperately needed in today's world. It is built on UNESCO's work to empower learners of all ages, providing them with the sense of empathy and solidarity to act as global citizens in line with the 2030 Agenda for Sustainable Development, in particular the Sustainable Development Goals 4 (on education) and 16 (to promote just, peaceful, and inclusive societies).

Specifically, the purpose of this manual is to provide a brief overview of approaches and tools for developing intercultural competencies and then to present in detail an adaptable practical tool called **Story Circles** that can be used in many different contexts and situations around the world for developing individuals' intercultural competencies. The manual concludes with an extensive list of resources that can be used in further intercultural training and development, as well as supporting materials that are helpful in facilitating Story Circles.

A brief comment on the words "context" and "appropriateness" in this manual: "Context" refers to the specific situation (in which Story Circles will be used), including the geographic location, the culture(s) within which the situation is located, the diverse backgrounds of the participants and facilitator; the political, economic, religious, and social factors of the situation; and the physical space. "Appropriateness" refers to the degree to which the interaction meets the social expectations of the people involved in the interaction. On additional note is that "methodology" refers to the entire process, while "tool" refers to the specific use of Story Circles.

The task

UNESCO is the lead agency for the International Decade for the Rapprochement of Cultures (2013–2022) within the UN system, as proclaimed by the UN General Assembly Resolution 67/104, adopted in December 2012. In line with UNESCO's mandate to build peace in the minds of men and women, it constitutes a follow-up to both the International Decade for a Culture of Peace and Non-violence for the Children of the World (2001–2010) and the International Year for the Rapprochement of Cultures (2010).

In 2013, recognizing the importance of enhancing the skills, attitudes, and behaviors of individuals for reaching the ambitions of the decade, UNESCO launched the publication *Intercultural Competencies: Conceptual and Operational Framework* (UNESCO, 2013b), providing a comprehensive overview of the importance of developing the capacities to manage growing cultural diversity and clarifying key related concepts and their operational interlinkages. The *Manual for Developing Intercultural Competencies* was, therefore, designed to translate this framework into a more tangible action and to propose a global, accessible methodology to help sensitize diverse audiences to key intercultural competencies, including *listening for understanding*, respect, cultural curiosity, empathy, and reflexivity.

Based on thorough research led by Dr. Darla K. Deardorff, the Story Circle methodology was identified and adapted for the purposes of developing a human rights–based approach to intercultural competencies. This methodology was successfully piloted in five regions: Thailand (for Asia and Pacific), Zimbabwe (for Africa), Costa Rica (for Latin America and Caribbean), Austria (for Europe), and Tunisia (for Arab States). The methodology is outlined in this manual. The pilots consisted of a train-the-trainers workshop organized by UNESCO, and then several newly trained facilitators led Story Circles within the local community. Following the pilots, the facilitators were interviewed, and, in addition, feedback was collected from focus groups on how effectively this tool contributed in developing further intercultural awareness and competencies. Two small pilots, based only on the Story Circles exercise, have also been led in Turkey and Vanuatu. We present throughout this publication texts from participants reporting their experiences with the methodology in these different regions. Overall, UNESCO determined that the methodology meets the criteria outlined in the earlier task. Follow-up information was received from participants several weeks out from the pilot on how effective they felt the Story Circles were in developing intercultural competencies and the progress made since then. The feedback and recommendations provided in these various ways were used to refine and update the Story Circles' process, including the specific prompts used in developing intercultural competencies through the sharing of personal experiences.

Overview of the manual

This manual is intended for trainers and those who are interested in developing intercultural competencies in others, particularly as part of intercultural dialogue, peace, and conflict resolution work; international development; and intercultural training and teambuilding. Grounded in theory (see p. 59) and written intentionally in more accessible language than many of the academic and government documents on intercultural competencies, this manual is a response to the task to identify a methodology for developing intercultural competencies in many different contexts around the world. This manual begins with a brief overview of intercultural competencies (recognizing that much work has already been done in this area). This is followed by a summary that highlights existing approaches and tools used in intercultural training as a way of contextualizing the selected tool, a description of the process used in selecting the Story Circles tool, and then a detailed description of the tool itself with instructions on how facilitators can use this methodology in developing intercultural competencies in various groups. The manual ends with further resources and supporting materials, including handouts that can be used with participants along with additional materials for facilitators (for criteria for facilitators, please see p. 79).

Defining intercultural competencies

To understand intercultural competencies and intercultural dialogue, it is first necessary to define culture. According to UNESCO,

> Culture is that set of distinctive spiritual, material, intellectual and emotional features of a society or social group, encompassing all the ways of being in that society; at a minimum, including art and literature, lifestyles, ways of living together, value systems, traditions, and beliefs.
>
> (UNESCO, 2001)

Each culture is the sum of assumptions and practices shared by members of a group, distinguishing them from other groups, and so one culture comes into clearest focus when compared to another culture maintaining different practices. However, cultures are themselves multiple so that to insiders, every group reveals itself not as homogeneous but rather a nested series of progressively smaller groups whose members are all too aware of distinctions between themselves. Cultures themselves are seldom the focus of attention in the discussion of intercultural competencies, for cultures have no existence apart from the people who construct and animate them. Thus members of cultural groups more adequately serve as the focus of attention.

What exactly are intercultural competencies and how can these competences be developed? There are many different definitions of intercultural competencies. UNESCO's 2013 publication entitled *Intercultural Competencies: Conceptual and Operational Framework* examined some of the emerging themes within intercultural competencies literature from different regions of the world. Based on that publication, the definition of intercultural competencies was broadly defined as

> adequate knowledge about particular cultures, as well as general knowledge about . . . issues arising when members of different cultures interact, holding receptive attitudes that encourage establishing and maintaining contact with diverse others, as well as having the skills required (in) . . . interacting with others from different cultures.
>
> (p. 16)

Some of the common elements of intercultural competencies across different cultures include respect, self-awareness/identity, seeing from other perspectives/worldviews, listening, adaptation, relationship building, and cultural humility (UNESCO, 2013b, p. 24). This 2013 publication included a visual conceptualization of the ways in which the many facets related to intercultural competencies fit together (see Figure 0.1 on p. xvi). A key part of the 2013 publication is an operational plan that outlines five steps for implementing intercultural competencies, including clarifying, teaching, promoting, and enacting intercultural competencies with specific activities that could be undertaken under each step. These activities are often reflective of organizational- or societal-level actions. This manual furthers the 2013 publication by outlining a tool in which to develop intercultural competencies at the individual level, recognizing that culture influences the societal expectations of individuals' behavior and communication that are considered appropriate within specific contexts. As Hall and colleagues (2012) note (p. 8), "It is important to view the acquisition of intercultural competencies as a learner-centred process," meaning that to develop intercultural competencies, it is important to start with individuals.

There are many definitions (and terms) of intercultural competencies, depending on the language and culture (see Deardorff, 2009; Spitzberg & Changnon, 2009 for examples). For instance, intercultural competencies, through a consensus definition, have also been defined as "communication and behavior that is both effective and appropriate when interacting across difference" (Deardorff, 2009; see Figure 2.1). Other definitions note the developmental stages of intercultural competencies (King and Baxter-Magolda, M. Bennett), the role of language (Byram), the importance of identity (Y. Y. Kim, Nwosu), and the role of mindfulness (Ting-Toomey) and motivation (Ting-Toomey, Gudykunst). Many of the definitions highlight specific knowledge, skill, and attitude dimensions of competences, and nearly all address differences between individuals. These competences are connected to, and even anchored in, human rights. In particular, the human rights principles of interrelatedness, equality, respect, dignity, participation, inclusion, and empowerment are all closely aligned with intercultural competencies (Donders & Laaksonen, 2014). To summarize many existing definitions, *intercultural competencies in essence are about improving human interactions across difference, whether within a society (differences due to age, gender, religion, socio-economic status, political affiliation, ethnicity, and so on) or across borders.*

For those who wish to understand more about the general context of intercultural competencies, there is an emerging body of literature on intercultural competencies (see the UNESCO, 2013b document on intercultural competencies along with books such as *The Sage Handbook of Intercultural Competence* and others listed at the end of this manual), although such work has been ongoing for over 50 years. Most of the academic work on intercultural competencies has originated from North America and Europe. UNESCO's *Intercultural Competencies* was one of the first documents that synthesized regional perspectives from around the world on this important concept, although there is still much work to be done in understanding intercultural competencies from a variety of perspectives.

Overview of approaches and tools for developing intercultural competencies

There are two main approaches to developing intercultural competencies: formal and informal/non-formal learning. **Formal intercultural learning** may occur through educational curriculum at all levels of schooling, specific short courses focused on particular elements of intercultural competencies, and formalized experiential learning opportunities (such as through job training or studying or working abroad). **Informal and non-formal learning opportunities** occur through exchanges; fine arts; cultural organizations; public spaces, such as museums and libraries; new media; and so on. Such learning also occurs through daily lived experience in interacting with those who differ in age, gender, religion, ethnicity, socio-economic status, political beliefs, or physical abilities, to name a few differences. Both approaches to developing intercultural competencies encompass the three main domains of learning to foster global citizenship education: cognitive, socio-emotional, and behavioral (UNESCO, 2015).[1] With the use of **technology**, intercultural materials are now available and accessible to many who may not need or have access to the formal learning context but may be motivated to engage in **self-directed learning**. Other **informal ways** of developing intercultural competencies include reading groups, film discussions, and theatrical productions, all three of which are forms of storytelling. All of these ways of developing intercultural competencies – formal, non-formal, informal, technology, self-directed – involve communication skills to some degree since, in the end, communication and behavior are at the center of intercultural competencies.

This overview focuses primarily on **specific intercultural training tools and activities** used predominantly in formal learning contexts (schools, courses, workshops, trainings) since these are targeted specifically at developing participants' intercultural competencies. It is important to note that research (Bennett, Deardorff) has shown that developing intercultural competencies is a lifelong process, so a one-time training or experience is insufficient if the goal is to *achieve* intercultural competencies. However, if the focus is on the *process* itself, then the goals of developing intercultural competencies become more realistic. More realistic intercultural goals can include practicing deep listening, increasing one's own cultural self-awareness, awareness of others, connecting across difference in a respectful manner, developing empathy, and discovering similarities, especially with those who seem quite different.

There are many different kinds of intercultural training tools used in a wide variety of settings (education, business, government, community development, and so on), including simulations, role plays, case studies, group activities, online tools, and coaching, all of which involve communication in some way. Most of these tools have been generated from Western paradigms and may not be contextually appropriate in non-Western settings. These intercultural training tools often take place in a more formal learning setting, such as a workshop or course and are usually facilitated by trainers who have a background knowledge of intercultural theories,[2] along with excellent facilitation skills. Generally, these tools should be used within a longer-term context, beyond one training time. There are pros and cons to each of these broad categories of intercultural training tools. (See Table 1.1 – note that this is not an exhaustive exploration of the pros/cons of each of these types of tools.) A general description of three of the key tool types follows.

Given the importance of experiential learning in intercultural competencies development, there are numerous intercultural **simulations** that have been developed. Simulations (including live action role-playing as a more elaborate type of simulation) allow for face-to-face interaction in a created reality in which to practice intercultural skills and behaviors but often require several hours to implement (and debrief) and may also require special materials, props, outfits, and physical space. Some of the classic simulations include BaFa BaFa[3] (Shirts, 1977), which usually takes about three hours to implement and Barnga, which is a type of card game that simulates cultural adaptation (Thiagarajan & Thiagarajan, 2011).

Group activities comprise a majority of training tools in developing intercultural competencies and these can often be found in intercultural activity books. For example, *Building Cultural Competence: Innovative Activities and Models* (edited by Berardo & Deardorff, 2012) features over 50 activities contributed from intercultural trainers from different countries. Areas of focus include exploring foundational cultural concepts, understanding differences, navigating identity, exploring cultural values that impact behavior, communicating successfully across cultural differences, building global teams, managing cultural transitions, and resolving differences. Other books of intercultural activities and tools include Council of Europe's *TASKs for Democracy: 60 Activities to Learn and Assess Transversal Attitudes, Skills, and Knowledge* and Stringer and Cassiday's *52 Activities for Improving Cross-Cultural Communication*. Examples of activities in these different books include role plays, creating visual collages, case studies, and

Table 1.1 Pros and cons of intercultural trainings tools

Types of Intercultural Training Tools	Pros	Cons
Simulations	Involves experiential learning, allows participants to experience differences and practice intercultural (IC) skills in a safe setting	Usually takes significant time (two to three plus hours); requires extensive debriefing from knowledgeable facilitators; may require particular materials, props, outfits, or space; and may cost money
Role plays	Involves experiential learning, allows participants to practice IC skills in a safe setting, provides a mechanism for generating feedback on communication/ behavior	May not be appropriate in some settings, requires participants to "perform" in front of others, requires careful development and selection of scenarios, requires thorough debriefing, requires a trained facilitator
Case studies	Provides concrete examples for discussion, engages participants through exploration of solution(s)	Requires careful development/ selection/wording of case studies, focuses primarily on the cognitive level of intercultural competencies (ICC) development
Group activities (games, discussions, structured learning exercises)	Can focus on particular aspects of ICC, engages in face-to-face interaction, allows for guidance and feedback from trained facilitator	Usually found in more formal settings, may require particular materials and space, requires skilled facilitator, needs to match activity with participants' learning styles
Online tools	Does not need to be in a formal learning setting, often utilizes self-directed learning, is available 24/7 with Internet access	There may be limited access to the Internet/computer; some online tools cost money; they have limited face-to-face contact; there is usually no guidance available; they are dependent on individual motivation
Coaching	Allows for tailored feedback on strengths and areas of continued intercultural growth	Requires a trained coach with a strong intercultural background; there are limited availability of such coaches; they often cost money

intercultural games. Many but not all of these intercultural activities and tools often utilize or require a particular room setup or specific materials, as well as trainers with a more formal background in intercultural theory.

In recent years, numerous **technological tools** have been developed online, such as Cultural Detective, Culture Vision used by some healthcare professionals; US Peace Corps interactive workbook, the first intercultural MOOC (Massive Open Online Course) in China, developed by Shanghai International Studies University; and so on. Newer technological tools may involve virtual and augmented reality (which requires special equipment). (Note: This is not meant to be a comprehensive list of available online intercultural tools but is rather meant to give a sampling of possibilities. And these are ones available in English – there are others available in different languages online around the world). These Internet-based tools, available 24/7, can aid in developing intercultural competencies and often incorporate reflexivity, which is a key part of intercultural competencies development. However, such tools need to be carefully evaluated as to the source of materials, the inherent biases that may be present, and the quality of the information presented (and to what extent the material is grounded in intercultural theory). In addition, such online tools often require a high degree of motivation from the individual and may lack formal guidance and feedback from an expert.

Regardless of the methods and tools used to develop intercultural competencies, **critical reflection** is a crucial part of the development process. What does critical reflection mean? Critical reflection involves critical thinking and includes three dimensions: a) making meaning of one's experience through descriptive, analytical, and critical considerations, which b) can be communicated in a number of ways, such as in written form, orally, or as an artistic expression, and c) then taking action based on one's reflection. UNESCO defines this as "the ability to step outside one's own experiences in order to reflect consciously upon them, considering what is happening, what it means, and how to respond" (UNESCO, 2013b, p. 17). Critical reflection is considered to be a precursor to transformation, which refers to a non-reversible shift in a person's perspective toward greater inclusiveness, openness, and flexibility, among other aspects of transformative learning (Mezirow, 1990). Specifically, critical reflection involves asking questions, such as, "What did I learn from this? What worked well, and what could be improved (in me)? What voices/perspectives are being represented? Whose voices are missing? What else would be helpful to know? What will I do with the knowledge/insights gained from this? As a result of this learning, what positive contributions can I make in my community and in civil society? How does this experience relate to other contexts, and how can this learning be applied in other settings?" Stepping back and engaging in this kind of deeper reflection is crucial in the development of intercultural competencies.

This brief overview demonstrates that there is much that already exists in regard to tools and activities for developing intercultural competencies. However, much of what exists often requires a facilitator/trainer with a strong background in intercultural theories (beyond lived intercultural experience) and often requires particular physical space, as well as special materials in order to implement these tools and activities. Many of these activities also lend themselves more to formal educational settings. This all means that there are certainly limits in being able to utilize the many existing intercultural training tools and activities, and, more importantly, the existing tools and activities do not fall within the parameters desired by UNESCO as previously noted in the initial charge and as outlined in the next paragraph.

Process for selecting a tool for developing intercultural competencies

The process for selecting a tool that can be used to develop intercultural competencies started with a review of existing intercultural training tools and mechanisms as just described in an effort to identify which tools might align best with parameters of this undertaking. Interviews and focus groups were conducted in numerous countries around the world, including China, Japan, the Netherlands, Italy, South Africa, and the United States, as well as with intercultural experts from different countries in regard to which intercultural training tools would work best in a wide variety of settings around the world to develop individuals' intercultural competencies. From these efforts, Story Circles emerged as an innovative adaptation of a long-standing tradition of sharing stories. Feedback on this manual was obtained from intercultural experts from Canada, Germany, Italy, Japan, China, the United States, and New Zealand; experts' feedback and suggestions were incorporated into this final document.

Notes

1 Global Citizenship Education aims to empower learners of all ages to assume active roles, both locally and globally, in building more peaceful, tolerant, inclusive, and secure societies and is based on three domains of learning: 1) cognitive: knowledge and thinking skills necessary to better understand the world and its complexities; 2) socio-emotional: values, attitudes, and social skills that enable

learners to develop affectively, psychosocially, and physically, and to enable them to live together with others respectfully and peacefully; and 3) behavioral: conduct, performance, practical application, and engagement.
2 Some of the key intercultural theories include those by Hofstede, Byram, Triandis, E. Hall, Bennett, and Deardorff, along with many others. Please see the list of resources at the end of this manual for more on intercultural theories.
3 BaFa BaFa replicates the experience of crossing cultural boundaries through the creation of two synthetic cultures.

2 Story Circles
Intercultural competencies development tool

"Story Circles" were designed as a practical intercultural tool for developing and practicing intercultural competencies that can be used with different groups of people in many settings around the world, that can be used outside of formal instructional settings, that uses little to no resources, and that can be facilitated by those who may not have a strong background in intercultural knowledge and theory. After careful examination of the existing intercultural tools, Story Circles were selected as the tool to feature in this manual for several reasons:

1) The 2013 UNESCO publication *Intercultural Competencies* noted the **importance and power of storytelling in many cultures** around the world throughout human time (even as indicated by the robust film industries in numerous countries around the world today). Further, the 2013 publication noted, "Only through joint construction of a relationship in which people listen to one another can individuals demonstrate their intercultural competencies" (p. 38), meaning that relationships (and listening) are very important in intercultural competencies development.

2) There is a long history of the use of storytelling in intercultural development. For example, DuBois wrote several books on a similar activity that was conducted nearly 100 years ago in the 1930s (see DuBois & Li, 1963; see also Arévalo-Guerrero, 2009; Holliday et al., 2010; Wang et al., 2017). Moreover, variations on Story Circles (or talking circles) have **existed in a range of cultural communities around the world** since ancient times and have been part of the human experience. In addition, Story Circles bring a more appropriate intercultural tool to settings where the predominant Western-developed intercultural tools may not be as suitable.

3) Story Circles focus on **fundamental elements of intercultural competencies** development, including **respect, listening, curiosity, self- and other awareness, reflection, sharing, empathy, and relationship building**.

4) Story Circles can be **easily adapted** to many different settings and contexts, depending on the prompts used, as well as being able to be adapted to any language.

5) Circle processes, defined as the process of a group of people sharing personal experiences in a circle, have already been **successfully used in numerous communities** around the world in bringing together those from different backgrounds, in resolving conflict, in improving social integration, and in truth and reconciliation processes (Pranis, 2005). Storytelling, on the other hand, is defined as a social and cultural activity of sharing non-fictional and fictional narratives as a means of entertainment, education, moral formation, or cultural preservation. Both circle processes and storytelling see stories as having the power to change behavior and reinforce values (Haven, 2007, 2014).

6) Circle processes provide a **non-threatening way in which individuals can share their personal experiences** and explore similarities, as well as differences, with each other. Based on intercultural theories (Bennett, 1993; King & Baxter-Magolda, 2005), many people are at the place of needing to explore similarities with those they perceive to be different from them, while some are at the place of being open to exploring differences. Story Circles, then, are developmentally appropriate for most people who would be participating.

7) Story Circles engage all three modes of learning: cognitive, socioemotional, and behavioral as a more holistic way of developing intercultural competencies. The key is in the emotional connections made with other participants through this methodology, which often do not happen with other more traditional intercultural training methods.

8) **Positive feedback** on the use of Story Circles to develop intercultural competencies has been received from intercultural experts, students, and local citizens from different cultures around the world, including in China, Japan, Canada, United States, Italy, Germany, Mexico, and South Africa. This feedback was collected through completed participant evaluations, focus groups, interviews, and observation.

Given the strong reasons outlined here, Story Circles have been identified as a tool that can work effectively in many different settings and with many different groups of people for *further developing intercultural competencies in individuals*.

Using Story Circles for developing intercultural competencies is an **innovative adaptation** of what could be considered even an ancient tradition of storytelling found in many cultures since it has not been used for this specific purpose until now. This manual, then, contributes to the existing body of intercultural training tools already noted by introducing an innovative adaptation that can be used in intercultural education and training, as well as in community development. Story Circles used intentionally for developing specific intercultural competencies is innovative, particularly in the use of specific intercultural prompts that guide the sharing of experiences and stories that focus on enhancing particular intercultural competencies dimensions. **This tool works for developing intercultural competencies only when used with a thorough debriefing/follow-up discussion** in which critical reflection is utilized (see previous section on critical reflection as well as the prompts, debriefing questions, and handout later in the manual).

Story Circles (also known as talking circles or peacemaking circles) bring people together into a situation of community where, based on the Story Circle process, everyone is respected and is considered equal and where participants are able to share more about themselves or a circumstance by telling their own stories based on their life experience. This sharing of personal experience not only validates the perspective of each individual but also generates new understandings and insights. In the Story Circles, life experience is highly valued as participants make themselves vulnerable in sharing stories of joy and pain as well as struggle and triumph, which engage participants on many levels including emotional, mental, spiritual, and even physical levels. While participants can decide their degree to which they wish to share (through the experience they choose to share, which can be a more meaningful or more surface-level experience), research has shown that vulnerability, based on mutuality, can be transformational (Brown, 2012). This begins with owning our stories and having the courage to share those.

Story Circles and intercultural competencies development

Story Circles provide a way for people from different backgrounds to come together to learn from each other and to explore cultural similarities and differences. Through the sharing of life experiences situated within specific cultural contexts, participants come to learn more about themselves, as well as their fellow humans, and through this process, participants further develop key elements of intercultural competencies, including greater self-awareness, openness, respect, reflexivity skills, empathy, increased awareness of others, and, in the end, greater cultural humility. Story Circles require one to be vulnerable enough to share one's own personal story, which is in itself a tool for reflection. Both self- and group reflections are essential to the process of developing intercultural competencies (see debriefing questions in the section that follows and in the handout at the back of this manual). The Story Circles experience becomes a tool for not only enhancing intercultural competencies development but also in deepening relationships with others and in emphasizing the interconnectedness of all.

Specifically, some **intercultural competencies goals** for Story Circles include the following: Demonstrating respect for others, practicing *listening for understanding*, cultivating curiosity about similarities and differences with others, gaining increased cultural self-awareness, developing empathy, and developing relationships with culturally different others.

Contexts of Story Circles

There are different types of Story Circles, including those for support, community-building, conflict, reintegration, and celebration. These have been used to augment the criminal justice system, address neighborhood disagreements, manage school classrooms, develop mission statements within organizations, resolve family conflicts, handle environmental and worker disputes, and facilitate dialogues within immigrant and host communities. However, Story Circles have not to date been used specifically for developing individuals' intercultural competencies, which is what makes this a new yet ancient tool for this purpose.

Specific situations in which Story Circles might prove useful in developing intercultural competencies include the following specific contexts:

1) **Teacher education** – teachers, students, parents, and/or school administrators come together to understand the unique perspectives of each in regard to teaching and learning expectations, impact of cultural contexts on education, and the realities of daily life impacting learning (see Zwicky, 2005).

2) **International projects** – project team members come together through Story Circles for teambuilding purposes, as well as to share their perspectives on what is important in working together successfully as a team, especially when project members are from different cultural, national, linguistic, and/or religious backgrounds.

3) **Community development** – diverse community citizens (of different ages, gender, religions, socio-economic backgrounds, etc.) come together to share their stories so as to create bonds and build relationships across generations, religions, and socio-economic backgrounds.

4) **Intercultural dialogue** – dialogue participants come together first through Story Circles to practice *listening for understanding* and

gaining insights on each other's perspectives before engaging in further dialogue across difference.

5) **Healthcare training** – patients and healthcare providers are brought together in understanding each other's perspectives and cultural contexts, as well as realities of addressing and navigating particular healthcare matters, whether a routine issue or serious illness.

6) **Police training** – police and community members (especially those representing minority populations) share stories from their own experiences in regard to concerns, conflicts, or issues plaguing the local community so as to enhance understanding from each other's perspectives and help enhance intercultural competencies, as well as improve relationships.

These are but a few of the specific contexts in which Story Circles can be used to develop individuals' intercultural competencies. There are many other contexts, including foreign language and intercultural education, religious contexts, and refugees contexts. Story Circles are also useful in further developing intercultural competencies by sharing different views on a significant local or global event and/or possibly moving toward collective action on issues of mutual interest/concern.

Description of Story Circles

Story Circles, simply put, involve the sharing of personal experiences within gatherings of three or more people. Based on an underlying value of the importance of human connection, Story Circles uphold **respect and openness as foundational aspects of any story circle**, both of which are fundamental in the development of intercultural competencies. Note that respect and openness must be upheld by all participants for the Story Circles experience to succeed. (See Table 2.1)

Story Circles operate on two presuppositions:

1) **We are all interconnected through human rights.**
2) **Each person has inherent dignity and worth.**

Table 2.1 Foundation of Story Circles

Foundation of Story Circles	
We are all interconnected through human rights.	Each person has inherent dignity and worth.
<RESPECT AND OPENNESS>	

Photo 2.1 Story Circles pilot in Bangkok, Thailand
Source: @UNESCO

**In addition to the two presuppositions, it is important
to remember that:**

a)   **Every person has personal experience that can be shared.**
b)   **We all have something to learn from others.**
c)   ***Listening for understanding* is transformational.**[1]

Story Circles can occur with three or more people, and generally take place in groups of four to five (usually no more than six to seven per group), regardless of the overall number of participants since the smaller groups help participants feel more comfortable in sharing. There are at least two rounds of stories shared, the first is a "get acquainted" round, and the second is a more substantive round that addresses intercultural competencies development. In each round, a prompt is given to which participants respond and the others in the circle *listen for understanding* (versus listening for response or judgment). *Listening for understanding* is crucial, as participants remain open to what they hear, how they ascribe meaning to what they hear, and how they "seek first to understand" instead of the more typical listening, which is in preparing a response, judging, or for determining one's position in relation to what is heard. After the two rounds of personal sharing/storytelling, the guided group reflection and discussion are crucial in moving forward toward enhanced intercultural competencies development for the participants. The total amount of time needed depends on the number of participants, but generally, a minimum of 75–90 minutes is recommended for a group of about 20–25, with the ideal time allotment being at least 120 minutes.

**Box 2.1   Building positive dialogue with youth
in Thailand**

Working with youth means creating safe spaces. When a group of young people has never met before, the kind of trust needed to be honest and open with others is a critical element essential for constructive outcomes. We need a methodology that enables people to build this type of trust by taking participants directly to personal experiences, common ground, and common values.

As a youth engagement specialist, one of the biggest challenges I face is how to bring such a diverse group of young people together and encourage open and honest dialogue. I see the "Manual for Developing Intercultural Competencies" as a tool that solves that challenge. Integrating this into UNESCO's work with young people will be indeed very useful.

I very much appreciated Darla's facilitation of the session in Bangkok using the Story Circles methodology. In a short space of time, a diverse group of people engaged in a relatively simple dialogue and was able to reach a level of openness and honesty that is all too rare. It did not require any fancy facilitation; it did not require the participants to have prior experience or technical knowledge. It is a methodology we can all recreate.

Young people in Asia and the Pacific are striving to build bridges toward a more peaceful and sustainable society. Over 800 young people were involved in the UN regional consultation on youth peace and security. UNESCO has identified more than 1,000 organizations in the region working with youth to implement the Sustainable Development Goals. Many of these organizations were founded by youth with a passion for contributing to their communities or the world.

Whilst the session in Bangkok brought together only around 30 young people, all of them are already involved in youth work. In addition to young people from Thailand, there were participants from across Asia, Latin America, and Europe – a truly diverse group. All of them are facilitators of change, especially through mobilizing other young people. The Story Circles methodology is now a tool all of them can use to further their individual efforts.

Adam Sharpe – former youth engagement specialist based in Bangkok, Thailand; former UNESCO coordinator of the Generation What Asia Pacific program from 2016–2018

Guidelines for using Story Circles

The following are some guidelines for using Story Circles in developing intercultural competencies:

• Be clear on the goals for using Story Circles, in this case, to enhance intercultural competencies development of the participants as they learn more about themselves and others in the circle and to deepen relationships. Note that Story Circles in this case are not meant to be used as therapy sessions or to pressure participants into consensus.

   Specifically, some intercultural competencies goals in Story Circle participation include the following (these can be adapted by the facilitators):

Story Circle goals related to intercultural competencies development

- **Demonstrate respect** for others
- **Practice *listening for understanding***
- **Cultivate curiosity** about similarities and differences with others
- **Gain increased cultural self-awareness**
- **Develop empathy**
- **Engage in critical reflection** on one's own intercultural competencies development, as well as on the intercultural experience
- **Develop relationships** with culturally different others

• Ensure the appropriateness and feasibility of using Story Circles. This means that participants are willing to be involved in this process (not coerced or forced), that participants are interested in developing their own intercultural competencies, that experienced facilitators are available, that there is a safe space for this process to occur, that there is sufficient time for the complete Story Circle process (including the personal sharing, as well as the follow-up discussion) and that this Story Circle process fits within societal and cultural expectations of what is considered appropriate.

- Affirm the equality[2] of all participants in the circle and the adherence to confidentiality in what is shared. (Confidentiality here means that what is shared within the groups is not to be repeated or shared with anyone else in any way unless permission is given first.)
- Create a safe space (physically, mentally, emotionally) in which all participants feel welcome and able to share their own truths and experiences in a climate of respect and dignity by having participants affirm the underlying presuppositions of interconnectedness and of all having inherent worth. (See the resources at the end of this manual for tips on creating safe space.)
- Allow for adequate debriefing/discussion time following the sharing of personal stories in the Story Circles. Learning and transformation (positive change toward increased intercultural competencies) occur as participants pause and reflect on what they have heard, why that new learning is important, and what they will do now as a result of the learning about themselves and others. Intentional guided reflection of this process by facilitators is very important (see the debriefing questions).

Conditions for using Story Circles in developing intercultural competencies

  *All participants are willing to be involved in the Story Circle process

  *Participants are interested in developing their intercultural competencies and understand that this is the purpose of the Story Circles experience

  *Participants uphold respect and openness toward all participants

  *Experienced facilitators are available to guide the Story Circle process

  *A safe space (physically, mentally, emotionally) for this Story Circle process to occur is provided

  *There is a commonly shared language in which to communicate

  *Sufficient time is allowed for the Story Circle process

  *Appropriateness for the societal and cultural expectations of the context is enforced

  *Participants adhere to confidentiality in what is shared

  *Participants affirm the equality of all in the circles

Note: When *not* to use Story Circles:

- When participants are unwilling
- When the topic of intercultural competencies development is not considered relevant to participants
- When there is not a common language that can be used and understood
- When there is a perceived inequality among participants (status, ethnicity, socio-economic level, etc.), *and* it is clear that participants will not be able to view all participants as equals at least while in the Story Circles. For more on this, including a possible solution, see the challenges section of the manual
- When the organizer is trying to convince others of a particular viewpoint or position
- When participants are not open to hearing and respecting perspectives different from their own
- When the intent is not respectful of all possible participants

Organizing a Story Circle

While there is no set way to organize a Story Circle, especially since the process may vary by context and setting, the following is a general outline of steps that can be taken to organize a Story Circle (adapted from Pranis, 2005):

1) Determine the purpose(s) of the Story Circle (in this case, to develop individuals' intercultural competencies through *listening for understanding* to others' stories of personal experience) – the purpose may also be tailored to the context and needs of participants. (See p. 20 for specific goals related to intercultural competencies development.)
2) Assess the suitability of the Story Circle process for the identified purpose of intercultural competencies development (see guidelines previously discussed).
3) Identify possible participants interested in developing their intercultural competencies (ensuring a variety of perspectives as much as possible – i.e., gender, age, religion, culture) – the more diverse the better the intended outcomes.
4) Determine the language that will be used for the Story Circles (based on which language is most accessible for ideally all of the participants, which may or may not be the first language for some of them). Note that all participants need to be able to communicate in a common language (or have accommodations made through interpretation).

5) Select the circle facilitator/co-facilitators (with the responsibility of maintaining a safe space for respectful dialogue, as well as welcoming participants, outlining the process, and guiding the discussion at the end).

6) Choose the appropriate time and place for the Story Circle (which should allow for chairs set in smaller circles, ideally with no furniture or barriers inside the circles, including no tables); participants may also sit in a circle on the floor, if that is appropriate, or even stand in a circle.

7) Extend invitations to possible interested participants that include the stated purpose, topic(s), and nature of the process (i.e., importance of *listening for understanding*, of respecting the other participants, and so on). It is very important that the invitation be framed explicitly as an opportunity to develop intercultural skills. The Story Circle should be referred to as an "experience" and not a "workshop" or "training" since that terminology sets up potentially unrealistic expectations.

8) Plan an appropriate opening and closing for the event, which will set an open and welcoming tone (could include a reading, deep breathing activities, music, etc.), will delineate the start and finish of the experience, and will be appropriate and understood by all participants.

9) Decide whether there will be a symbolic center piece in the circles (such as flowers) and if food will be involved either at the beginning or end of the circle experience. (Note: Food at the beginning can serve to help participants feel more comfortable as they begin to get to know each other.) Also, determine if "talking pieces" are to be used in the circles (and if so, provide an *appropriate* "talking piece" that will be acceptable to all participants).

10) Select the prompts to be used (see the examples that follow). You will need one "get acquainted" prompt for the first round and one intercultural competencies prompt for the second round. These prompts should be selected based on the specific intercultural goals for the Story Circle as well as appropriateness for the context and participants. Note: Selection of the appropriate prompts (see the list in this manual) is very important. These prompts can also be adapted or even created to fit the context as long as they align with the criteria outlined in part III item IIIB.

11) Determine the debriefing questions to be used after the story process and be prepared to facilitate the whole group reflection/discussion.

12) Arrive early to ensure that the space is adequately and appropriately prepared.

Photo 2.2 Story Circles pilot in Harare, Zimbabwe
Source: ©Winston Chaniwa/Afriphotos

Note: Depending on the context, "Story Circles" can use other names, given what is most appropriate to the particular context. Possibilities could include Crossroads, Learning from Each Other, Sharing through Experiences, and Intergroup Connection.

**Box 2.2   The power of Story Circles fostering peace
in Zimbabwe communities**

The pilot in Harare, Zimbabwe, attested that Story Circles is a useful methodology, which provided young people, from different backgrounds, with an opportunity to discuss a number of issues, using stories drawn from their personal experiences. The participatory nature of the methodology allowed young women and men to share their thoughts and personal experiences, and deepen their commitments to build peaceful societies.

These efforts have contributed to tolerance among young people from different religions, political views, cultural values, and beliefs, thereby reducing misunderstandings, conflict, and violence, especially for the politically volatile areas such as Ushewokunze.

One would think the methodology would end with participants sharing their lived experiences. However, the experience brought out that it does not end with them just understanding each other; the methodology also challenged participants to consider how they would hold each other to account for the commitments they had made and what they would do with the knowledge they had gained. Furthermore, the commitment phase also ensured that the participants listened attentively throughout the process.

Manuel Kazamento is a young man aged 25 who lives in Mufakose. He noticed that young people in Zimbabwe are faced with high levels of unemployment and little entrepreneurship opportunities, which in many cases have resulted in a pool of frustrated and bitter young citizens with no hope of a better future. He pointed out that some of them are no longer keen to even participate in elections. Most of the young women and men in peri-urban and high-density suburbs of Harare had been involved in acts of violence during the earlier electoral process.

Intervention

Manuel Kazamento was introduced to the Story Circles methodology on intercultural competencies by his friend, who had participated in the first session conducted in Mufakose. He attended three sessions focusing on empathy, relation-building, and self-awareness. Manuel said the reflection and debriefing after each session was very effective, as he was able to assess the connections between his story and those of others participants, and identify the changes needed to address diversity in the future. Through this process, Manuel has come to appreciate the differences in individuals and the need for empathy and tolerance in resolving conflicts and misunderstandings. In his own words,

"The intercultural competence development dialogues have changed my view towards people with different cultures and political views. I now recognize that diversity is a strength which ought to be celebrated and accepted in human societies if we are to live peacefully."

Results

Through the intercultural competence he gained, Manuel is challenging other young people who also participated in the dialogue sessions to spread the message of peace and tolerance. He believes that if more young people are empowered with these skills, they will appreciate individuals, irrespective of their different political views. He has also invited other young women and men who were former perpetrators of violence to attend the sessions in order to empower them with inter-cultural competencies skills and promote reconciliation, fostering a culture of peace in their communities.

Farai Muronzi – Hub Director of Restless Development*

----

*Restless Development is a youth-led development founded in 1985 that currently works in India, Nepal, Sierra Leone, South Africa, Tanzania, Uganda, Zambia, and Zimbabwe, and has offices in London and New York. Its mission is to place young people at the forefront of change and development.

The role of the facilitator

The role of facilitators in Story Circles is to introduce the process, provide instructions on the process (see the following), to organize the participants into small groups, to be available if any questions or issues arise while small groups are engaged in the Story Circle process, and to facilitate the debrief of the experience. Note that it is important for facilitators to remain separate from the small groups and to *not* be a member of the small groups since this impacts the power dynamic in the group. It is strongly recommended that there be co-facilitators for these Story Circles experiences so that the co-facilitators together can help maintain and ensure a safe space, and address any issues that may arise among participants.

Facilitation instructions

Here are detailed facilitation instructions (note that this process itself is simpler in practice than what appears here due to the level of detail provided). There is scope for pedagogical interpretation on behalf of the facilitator/co-facilitators based on the following:

1) Welcome participants as they arrive in the manner appropriate to the participants (that meets their expectations of "welcome").
2) Invite participants to be seated in one large circle.
3) Begin with words of welcome and the selected method for focusing participants (i.e., reading, music). This initial introduction (including steps 4–7) is crucial for not only setting expectations and framing the

overall experience but also in creating a safe space for everyone and for marking the beginning of the experience.

4) Review the Story Circle process with the whole group, including the purpose, intent, and goals.

5) Develop guidelines/ground rules together as a group. These guidelines/ ground rules should be recorded in some way so that all participants can see them throughout the Story Circle experience. In developing guidelines, ask participants how they want to characterize this process (what will help make it safe and successful for them?), and remind the group of the importance of maintaining confidentiality and of speaking the truth from their own perspectives/experiences, as well as the importance of *listening for understanding* to what is shared (instead of listening for judgment or for response). Ask participants to identify promises they would like from other participants to make the circle a place where they can feel safe. (See "Creating a Safe Space" at the end of this manual for important ground rules to include.) Emphasize that it is important for each group member to commit to upholding these guidelines and that it is up to group members to hold each other accountable. Note that a handout can also be used, which contains guideline/ground rules, as long as the facilitator asks for any additions (see p. 71 for a sample handout).

6) As part of the guidelines/ground rules, it is important to emphasize confidentiality and respect. It is also important to mention that as each person shares his/her story, the others in the group are to *listen for understanding* and *not* interrupt the story (by asking questions or making comments) until all stories have been told (this also means refraining from asking clarification questions until after all stories have been shared, at which time some clarifying questions may be asked). Not interrupting is a way to demonstrate respect for the person sharing and forces the listeners to listen more closely to what is being shared. Participants in the group should not be distracted by electronic devices or in other ways, unless to take a few brief notes on the memorable point from each story for the "flashback" time that follows, once all stories have been shared.

7) Story Circles is very structured in the way of time limits (see the following for further details on time parameters). The purpose of the time limits is to ensure equality of all participants and to make sure that each person in the group has the same amount of allotted time. Be sure to explain the purpose for the time parameters and ask participants to take responsibility for observing these time parameters. Instruct that the person to the right of the storyteller should be the timekeeper and decide in advance as a whole group what appropriate non-verbal signal

will be used to indicate that there is no more time left. (In some settings, it may be possible to extend the time parameters and for participants to share longer as long as all participants have the same amount of time. It is important to agree in advance on the time parameters as a whole larger group.) Note again that group members need to hold themselves and each other accountable in regard to the time parameters so that all have equal amounts of time.

8) Have participants divide into smaller groups (ideally in groups of five to six – with no fewer than four and no more than seven) for the actual sharing of personal experience. Smaller groups help participants feel less intimidated in sharing their personal stories, plus smaller groups are more efficient timewise. These smaller groups can be divided randomly or more intentionally, depending on the context. If appropriate, these smaller groups can involve those of different ages, status, genders, religious backgrounds, hometowns, and so on. The important piece to remember when groups are divided is that the groups should *be as diverse as possible* so that the members are able to share and learn from *diverse* perspectives. Very important: Participants are to remain in the same small groups for the entire experience (unless there is some unforeseen reason why the groups need to change, and if that happens, the entire process would need to start over) – do not allow participants to keep switching to new groups since it is important to maintain trust and confidentiality and a sense of safety within the same small group.

9) Remind participants that this particular story sharing should involve the following:

- **Be yourself;**
- **Maintain confidentiality;**
- **Speak from your own experience only;**
- **Be genuine and authentic;**
- **Keep your sharing simple, clear, and focused;**
- **Uphold positive intent;**
- **Be comfortable in your own style (i.e., sit, stand, use gestures); and**
- **Talk with others in your group as a fellow human.**

(Denning, 2005)

10) Begin with the first round, sharing the prompt/question to be answered and modeling an appropriate response for the participants. Modeling the appropriate response from the facilitator is very important, especially in helping participants know expectations for sharing.

11) It may be helpful to give participants a minute or two of silence to think about their responses to the prompt and what stories they want to share so that once participants begin sharing their stories, the focus can be on truly *listening for understanding* (instead of still trying to think of one's own story to share). Remind participants again about not interrupting when someone else is speaking in order to foster respectful deep listening.

12) Once the stories from the first round have been shared, groups can move into the personal stories for the second prompt.

The facilitator may want to allow a few minutes for participants to reflect first on the question/prompt individually (especially if this is not participants' first language) before sharing in the small group.

13) Begin the second round by sharing the intercultural prompt/question to be answered and modeling an appropriate response for the participants (modeling by the facilitator is very important, including for the facilitator to model vulnerability and the courage to share personally). The purpose of this intercultural prompt is to have participants reflect on their own personal experiences with those who are different from them and share an experience so that the others in the group can begin to see from different perspectives. Again, it may be good to allow one to two minutes of silence while participants think of an experience to share. Remind participants not to interrupt the storyteller with questions or comments.

14) Once the stories/experiences from the second round have been shared, then participants engage in a flashback in response to the shared stories. The purpose of the flashback is to demonstrate *listening for understanding*, demonstrate respect, and make connections (all part of intercultural competencies development). The flashback involves participants sharing quickly in 15 seconds or less **the most memorable point** they heard from the second story shared. To do this, the group starts with the first person who shared his/her story in round two, and the others go around the circle to tell that person the most memorable point of his/her story. Then the group moves to the second person who shared his/her story and the others do another round of flashbacks for that person, and so on until the flashbacks have been covered for each person in the circle. This should be a relatively quick activity that does not devolve into discussion. Note: It is important to not skip this part, as it is a very important part of the Story Circles experience in demonstrating respect and *listening for understanding* each participant in the Story Circle, as well as making connections. Further, this flashback time can be a transformational experience for participants. Regarding time: This

is intentionally meant to be kept short – only 15 seconds or less per flashback. If there is ample time and if appropriate, this time could be extended. However, it is important to ensure that each person has equal amounts of time.   ⸱

15) After the flashbacks are finished, the small group can begin the debriefing/follow-up discussion using the suggested debriefing questions that follow. (The debriefing questions can be used as a handout, found at the end of this manual in part III.) Participants may need time for written reflections prior to discussing the debriefing questions (for example, if they are engaging in a language other than their first language) before sharing in the larger group. Participants may also feel most comfortable discussing some of these debriefing questions first in their smaller groups before rejoining the larger whole group circle for further follow-up discussion. After small groups have the opportunity to discuss a few of the key debriefing questions, then bring all the small groups back together as a whole group again and discuss some of the debriefing questions together, reminding participants to maintain confidentiality by not sharing names or details in the whole group. Note: This debriefing time is absolutely crucial for reflecting on how this methodology helped participants meet the goals related to intercultural competencies development, such as practicing *listening for understanding*.

16) Throughout the two rounds, monitor the process to ensure that there is no interrupting/responding during the stories, that each group member gets adequate time, or that there is no disrespect in any way. If any of this happens, temporarily suspend the sharing to revisit the guidelines and ask if participants can recommit to these guidelines or if there are changes that need to be made. It may also be good to introduce the idea of a "talking piece" that can be used only when someone is talking, which is an object that is passed around and only the person holding the object can speak. The use of a "talking piece" is a strongly recommended practice within Story Circles, and especially with younger participants. (See the challenges section for further description and discussion on this.)

17) Following the whole group debriefing/discussion and reflection, which is crucial to this process, invite participants to share any closing remarks or comments. A possible prompt for this is to invite participants to share their most significant intercultural learning or insight from the day.

18) Once participants have shared, then the facilitator(s) may wish to have them complete a written evaluation/reflection of the experience. This is also the time for the facilitator to engage participants in a discussion on

possible follow-up and next steps (on completing an action plan found at the end of the manual, on continuing to develop one's intercultural competencies and/or in maintaining relationships). The facilitator then makes closing remarks that could include general observations on what has been achieved by the group (i.e., noting the commonalities within human experiences, the increased awareness, and other themes that emerged from discussions). Thank everyone for participating and for committing to the respectful process. End by reminding participants of their interconnectedness and how intercultural competencies development is a lifelong process. The facilitator(s) may want to use music again (or a reading) to end the experience.

Note that these steps should not be considered rigid and need to be adapted to each context, although there are essential elements, such as the development of guidelines/ground rules as a group, as well as emphasizing the importance of respect of all participants, of equality within the group, and *listening for understanding.*

Photo 2.3 Story Circles pilot in San José, Costa Rica
Source: ©UNESCO

Box 2.3   Implementing Story Circles with indigenous peoples in Costa Rica

Intercultural skills are necessary in a globalized world where we see increasing threats to human rights. They are key to developing skills to make communication and exchange possible among the many different actors involved. We live in a very diverse world where every day we have to deal with people who are different from us. Intercultural competencies are life skills, necessary for individuals to exchange with people from other backgrounds and cultures.

I was impressed by Story Circles, as they seemed to establish an enriching dynamic from the outset.

My experience with this methodology can be divided in two: at first, I participated in the pilot, and then I applied the methodology in my field of work.

I believe the success of the pilot is due to the genuine interest of the participants. Although the activity lasted for several hours, people were extremely comfortable sharing their stories. No one wanted to break the Story Circle even though the activity time was over. This was a powerful result from such a short experience.

I then went on to implement Story Circles in a meeting of indigenous women leaders organized by my non-governmental organization (NGO). I thought this tool could be very useful in the context of a meeting with 30 women leaders. They all had different mother tongues and came from three different indigenous peoples – ngäbe, bribri, and cabécares – yet they shared a lot as leaders of their communities.

I decided to use the prompt focusing on the origin of the name of the participants. The tool was well received, especially because the name of bribris and cabécares peoples are derived from their clans. The women were happy to share with their indigenous sisters (as they are used to saying) the history of their clans.

This experience showed me that people have in common many more things than they might initially believe. During the Story Circle, there was space for true exchange, with participants listening and connecting to each other with respect, even though they were different. When we shared our stories, it was easy to empathize with participants. It can be said to create solidarity and brotherhood, as well as a greater sense of humanity.

Luciana Batalla Bunn – member of a Costa Rica's Indigenous NGO

Participating in the Latin American pilot of the UNESCO Manual for Developing Intercultural Competence was undoubtedly an interesting and at the same time challenging experience.

At first, the idea of a training to put the Story Circles methodology into practice was received with skepticism. As the process went on an interesting and rich exchange of experiences between people of very different contexts and ages, but with common concerns about the defense of human rights in intercultural environments, took place. For me, this was an opportunity to reiterate that every person has something to tell and that deserves to be shared, and they can learn from other experiences.

Learning the skill of active listening was unique, as it enabled cultural openness. People did not know each other, but each one gave time, respect, and importance to every shared story.

As a facilitator, I noticed how the groups began to create their own synergies, their own dynamics, appropriating the methodology in this unique Latin American context. A process of empathy and closeness between people was unleashed through intimate stories and comments. Although people lived in different contexts, they had in common realities of inequality and inequity, as well as hope in the future. It was surprising to hear from indigenous natives that Story Circles embody some of the same qualities that are used in other communication mechanisms within the indigenous communities in the country.

The fact that the Costa Rica pilot would inspire the implementation of the methodology in other communities in the Latin America region was especially appreciated and contributed to the success of the experience.

In this regard, challenges and lessons were raised on how to implement in the future the Story Circles methodology, in particular among young populations in situations of vulnerability and among indigenous communities in Latin America and the Caribbean. It seems important, given the existing inequalities, to cover the basic needs of participants. It also seems appropriate to communicate clearly to the group and adapt the training and materials for illiterate people who are not accustomed to reading/writing or for groups that speak diverse languages, as well as avoiding any dichotomy or structure of power between "facilitator/participant." At the same time, we must take into account the diversity of existing worldviews. For indigenous people, for instance, the limitation of time does not belong to the domain of the human, but to Mother Nature. In short,

> it is necessary to continue to readapt tools for building dialogue and peace where they are most necessary, in heterogeneous groups, so that cultural diversity can be appreciated in our societies as a source of wealth, not as a threat, and as links of multiple unions that can live in peace.
>
> *Maria del Mar Obando Boza – writer/philosopher,*
> *founder of a philosophy program for children*

Story Circle prompts examples (to be used in the same smaller group)

First "get acquainted" round

The following are examples of prompts; the facilitator would only use one. The main goal of this first round is to help participants meet each other, begin to build trust, and begin to feel comfortable sharing with each other interculturally (meaning that they begin to reveal something about their own backgrounds with a prompt that is directed more at pleasurable topics, such as food, holidays, and so on). Note that even if participants already know each other, it is still helpful to use a "get acquainted" prompt to build trust within the smaller circles.

1) Please tell us your name and the story about your name. (What does it mean? How did you come to have this name?)
2) Please tell us your name and three words or phrases that describe your background, and why those words/phrases are important to you.
3) Please tell us about an object or photo that you brought with you that tells us something about you and your background.
4) What is your favorite holiday or festival, and why is this your favorite?
5) What is a favorite food you would eat growing up and how does that relate to your background?

Second "intercultural competencies" round

The following are examples of intercultural prompts; the facilitator would only use one, although if there is sufficient time to engage in the "flashback" after each prompt plus debrief time, then a second prompt could be used. Note that it is important that the selected prompt be aligned with the desired overall outcome of further intercultural competencies development (see the specific goals listed on p. 20).

1) What is one of the most positive interactions you have had with a person(s) who is different from you, and what made this such a positive experience?
2) What is your earliest memory of difference (when you first learned or realized that you were different from someone else)?
3) What is a memorable experience you have had with a person(s) who is different from you (age, religion, gender, socio-economic, culture, nationality, etc.), and what did you learn about yourself and/or the other person in that experience?
4) What is one of the more challenging interactions you have had with a person(s) from a different background, and what did you learn from this?
5) What is a memorable cultural misunderstanding you have had, and what did you learn from this?
6) Describe someone who you know personally or who is known to you (via media, in history, etc.) that you feel can get along well with others, especially those who are different from that person. What is it that helps that person get along with others?
7) Describe a time when you realized you believed in a stereotype (about a group you are part of *or* a group that you are not part of) that was not true? What happened?
8) Describe a leader who seems to relate well to people from many different backgrounds. What are the qualities that you admire in this person and why? Which of these qualities are important for positive interactions with others?
9) What is a metaphor from your own experience that illustrates how a cultural clash can be overcome?
10) Describe a time when you felt supported by a community (of friends, colleagues, family members, neighbors). How would you describe this community in terms of similarities and differences, and how did this community demonstrate support?

Debriefing/discussion questions

Story Circles should only be used if there is adequate time for the debriefing/discussion that follows (a minimum of 30 minutes of debriefing time is recommended). Debriefing is an integral part of the Story Circle experience and is key in supporting the development of intercultural competencies, in particular because of the value of "stepping back" and reflecting on the process itself and in learning from that process. Debriefing/discussion can occur first within the smaller Story Circle groups and then later as the whole group, or start off as a whole group, depending on what would work best in each particular situation. Often, debriefing/ discussion works well by using a combination of the smaller group and larger group formats.

The following are some debriefing/discussion questions that can be used in facilitating and guiding group discussion following the sharing of stories. This broader group reflection is very important to the overall Story Circle process. (Note that if the group is too large, it might be good to divide the group into smaller groups of 20 or less so more participants have the opportunity to share or to continue sharing in the original smaller Story Circle groups at least in the beginning before coming together as the larger group). Selected discussion prompts should help participants work toward the desired overall outcome of intercultural competencies development. Note that these questions can also be found as a handout at the end of this manual (facilitators could have participants answer all of the questions or indicate which ones they should reflect on and discuss). The questions with an asterisk are very important to include in the debriefing since they address the intercultural competencies goals.

1) What is memorable to you in what you heard?
2) What surprised you?
3) What challenged you in the stories you heard?
4) *What did you learn about yourself through this experience (this refers to the goal of increased cultural self-awareness)?
5) *What common themes did you hear from the stories?
6) *What do you want to explore further after hearing these stories? What are you curious about, or what do you want to learn more about regarding similarities and differences with others (this refers to the goal of cultivating curiosity about similarities and differences with others)?
7) *How has this experience helped you practice *listening for understanding? In developing empathy (this refers to the listening goal related to developing intercultural competencies)?*
8) Complete this statement: I used to think . . . now I think . . .
9) *Stepping back from the experience itself, what are one to two insights you've gained that will help you relate better to those who are different from you?
10) *What will you do now as a result of this experience?
11) How has this larger group discussion helped you gain further intercultural insights about improving relationships we have with those who are different from us?

12) As a result of this learning, what positive contributions can we make in our communities and in civil society?

Variations on the group discussion/debriefing at the end of the story sharing include the following if the parameters of the setting and context allow for such:

a) Participants can be given a blank sheet of paper and asked to reflect on some of the earlier questions and then write their responses briefly. This can be especially helpful if not everyone has the same first language, as this gives time to think more carefully in a language other than one's first language. The questions are already included in a handout at the end of this manual if the facilitator would prefer to use it and instruct participants as to which questions they should respond.

b) Participants can be put in groups of three to five (these can be the same groups or new groups could be formed) and asked to create a poster collage (with actual magazine pictures or even drawn pictures) that represent the intercultural learning that occurred during the experience (for example, each person selects one or more pictures that represents his/her own intercultural learning about self and others from the experience). These posters can then be presented to the whole group. Participants may also wish to select and share a song that represents the intercultural learning that occurred. Other creative arts methods can also be used, such as human sculpture, spoken word, poetry, or role plays.

c) Participants can be put into groups of three to five and asked to write key learnings on slips of paper that can then be collected and redistributed for review; each group is asked to select the top two through consensus that represent the overall learning from this experience. Each group then presents these top-two learnings to the entire group.

d) For further follow-up, participants can be asked to develop an action plan in which they identify elements of intercultural competencies they would like to focus on next, list what they will do to enhance those elements specifically, and state how they will continue to engage with those who are different from them (see the action plan handout at the end of this manual). This can be especially useful if the facilitator meets individually with participants later as a follow-up to the Story Circle experience.

Photo 2.4 Story Circles pilot in Vienna, Austria
Source: ©UNESCO

**Box 2.4   Strengthening relatedness through active
listening and trust: Story Circles experience at
an Austrian school**

As a trainer for the Austrian Integration Fund (Österreichischer Integrationsfonds – ÖIF), I have to deal with the challenge arising from the various backgrounds and cultures of new arrivers to my country. This makes intercultural competencies essential for successful integration into the Austrian society.

In this regard, Story Circles can be a helpful tool to focus more on similarities than on differences, while also enhancing skills for communicating across difference, in particular the skill of *listening for understanding*: It happens quite often that people just talk to each other and forget the crucial part of effective communication: the listening. This method explicitly focuses attention on what the other participants say, a useful but challenging novelty.

There is no doubt that Story Circles bring people together easily. The small group size (four to five people) helps to create a friendly environment so that the participants feel comfortable opening up. Very soon, it becomes obvious that the parts of our personal history that we have in common are much bigger than the ones that separate us.

Our Story Circle took place in a public school in Vienna. The participants were pupils aged between 12 and 15. We had two groups: one in the morning and one in the afternoon.

Quite soon, we realized that there would be great differences between our own experience (as adults working in the field of integration) and that of the young people. First of all, we had to adapt the handouts, the rules, and the program to our audience. Second, the expectations were different, and the language issues were challenging.

The classes had a majority of pupils with a mother tongue other than German, and some of them had been living in Austria only for a short period.

To put it in a nutshell, every group is unique and so should be the way we implement the methodology.

The pupils realized that the classmates they already knew had new stories to tell and new aspects of their lives to share. I also had the feeling that the activity had an impact on the way they see their own group. They appeared to be more united and mature after the session. It was really important for them to make sure the trainers could not hear their conversations, for example. They took the sessions quite seriously.

As advice for those who will apply the activity in the future, I would recommend that before launching the Story Circles in a particular context, basic information about the participants should be obtained, including their language skills, in order to determine a common working language. There is no need to have details, especially not about their position/role in the class; however, having some background information will help to prepare the material and to provide some guidance for the composition of groups. Furthermore, I would recommend carrying out the session in the morning, as concentration is much lower in the afternoon.

For pupil groups, it would be helpful to adjust the timeline and the material (schedule, rules, and feedback). I believe that the pupils ask and act more freely if the trainer is not the teacher, and it would be appropriate to use hourglasses or clocks without sound for timekeeping. For our group, the communication tools had to be simplified and visible. We created posters with the main rules, and we kept reminding the students of these rules as the session advanced. We explained every step several times due to concentration capacities in this specific age group, and we split the steps to have more time control about the groups.

Iris Rehklau, trainer for the Austrian Integration Fund*

*The Austrian Integration Fund (ÖIF) aims at providing language, professional, and social integration of asylum beneficiaries and migrants on the basis of their respective rights and obligations in Austria.

We are living in times when societies and, consequently, school environments are contentious and individualistic, and I believe that taking part in narratives from other cultures broadens the minds of pupils and opens them up for new things they do not yet know about. The pilot undertaken at our school has shown quite well that the pupils are not open enough to other cultures and that much action is required in this respect. From my point of view, the Story Circle tool is a very good way of enabling pupils to think outside the box.

During the Story Circle activity, we experienced the pupils from a completely different angle than in a normal classroom situation. The pupils got the opportunity to know each other better, especially those who had never shared their personal experiences. Through active listening and applying the principle of trust, a unique dynamic emerged in the groups.

I was especially impressed by the moment when students asked me not to listen to them because they just wanted to share their stories within the group. I think that this welds a group together and fosters dynamic relationships. It was also very memorable when a pupil confessed that he had never received support in his life. This is how we get to know the pupils better and can strengthen our relationship, which is crucial for the learning process. Learning is only possible through relatedness.

Anna Haase – teacher of the Franz Jonas Europaschule

Anticipating challenges in using Story Circles

Some challenges that may arise in using Story Circles include the following:

1) One of the biggest challenges is ensuring that group participants just listen (for understanding) and *not* respond verbally to the stories that are told by commenting or asking questions. It is often natural for listeners to want to comment on a story or to ask questions, especially for clarification, but there should be no verbal responses until all stories in the group have been told. One way to counteract this is to use something like a "talking piece" (this could be a rock, a stick, a book, a piece of fruit, a pencil – whatever object is designated as the "talking piece" – noting that the more meaning a "talking piece" has to the participants, the more it will add to respecting the overall process) that is passed to and held by the person telling the story. Only the person holding the "talking piece" may speak. When the person has finished telling the story, the "talking piece" is passed to the next person, who then begins telling his or her story. In providing such a concrete visual object as a reminder, this often works quite well in eliminating talking from others and eliminating "dominating" by one individual, and helps to be a common thread that connects all in the circle.

2) Language, as previously noted, may be a challenge for some participants if they are having to share in a language other than their first language. Facilitators should be aware of this challenge and possibly consider the following measures if appropriate: provide the prompts in writing as well as saying them to the group; allow time for participants to think about their response to the prompts (and even make some written notes); encourage use of drawing or other visual pictures in the sharing of personal experiences. The same would be followed in the debriefing/discussion.

3) Another challenge that may arise is in using prompts that elicit deeper emotions or conflicts, which means a more skilled facilitator should be present to navigate through the deeper emotions that may surface. Conversely, if there are co-facilitators, one of the facilitators can work one-on-one with any in the group who are overwhelmed by emotion – usually separate from the group – while the other facilitator continues on with the Story Circle experience. Be sure to select prompts very carefully and ensure a) suitability and appropriateness for the group and b) prompts match the skill level of the facilitator.

4) Vulnerability may become an issue in some contexts since storytelling of one's personal experiences requires a degree of vulnerability and perhaps even courage. It is important for the facilitator to be aware of

this and to also ensure the creation of a "safe space" in which to share these personal stories (see tips for creating safe space at the end of this manual for more on this). Often, starting with the "easier" prompt is a good way for participants to get to know each other, to begin to establish trust, and to become more comfortable delving further into personal experience. If needed and possible, the two rounds of the Story Circle could occur in separate meetings to allow more time for participants to get to know each other and to build trust. For example, the first meeting could involve more of an initial "icebreaker" followed by round one and then the second meeting could involve round two. In some circumstances, meeting multiple times would help participants build relationships and trust, as well as to continue to develop intercultural competencies over time. It is important to remember that vulnerability, defined as "uncertainty, risk and emotional exposure" (Brown, 2012, p. 34) takes courage, respect, and mutuality. Vulnerability is not to be confused with weakness but rather vulnerability is strength, truth, and genuineness (Brown, 2012). Vulnerability is woven through life experiences, and interpersonal connection requires a degree of vulnerability.

5) Resistance may be another issue if participants resist storytelling or sharing their personal experience. Such resistance can occur for a variety of reasons, including misaligned expectations (especially if the invitation/publicity did not accurately state the purpose and goals), discomfort (especially at disclosing more personal experiences, in which case a more generic, less threatening prompt may be selected), awkwardness in being in the presence of others who may have previously been in conflict, personality or cultural factors (for example, if someone is an introvert), unwillingness to use the structured methodology as instructed (some may prefer to switch to more of a group discussion which – while more comfortable for some – is not recommended since group discussion does not achieve the stated intercultural goals, including *listening for understanding*) or often, the basis for resistance is fear. Sometimes, resistance may even be due to perceived bias from the facilitator toward some participants (or favoring those from the same background as the facilitator). The facilitator first needs to make sure that the stated purpose and goals of the Story Circle experience are very clear and understood by all participants and that all participants are committed to upholding the manual guidelines discussed. The facilitator also needs to determine how to reduce anxiety and focus on creating a safe environment for sharing. Creating a safe environment may involve preparation to understand the participants better, their needs, and their concerns, as well as ensuring a safe and welcoming physical space for the Story Circles (see tips for creating safe space at the end of

this manual, adapted from Chaitlin, 2003), and even meeting multiple times in order to build relationships with and among participants. It is also important to refer back to the section on when *not* to use Story Circles, including mandating or requiring participation, which often leads directly to resistance from reluctant participants. (For more on dealing with resistance, as well as other key aspects of intercultural facilitation, see Bennett, 2012).

6) A possible challenge in bringing participants together may be the perceived status variances of the participants due to age, job title, family name, socio-economic status, or other reasons, all of which depends on the specific context. It is also important for participants to embrace human rights as a compass for the use of Story Circles. If participants are not able to embrace the two presuppositions that we are all connected through human rights and that all persons have inherent worth and dignity, then the Story Circle process should be reconsidered. Further, it is important to recognize that Story Circles engender equality (meaning everyone has the same status, role, and rights within the Story Circle space), and that it may be potentially awkward for some participants to share and participate fully. The initial welcome and framing instructions from the facilitator become even more important in helping all feel comfortable. If status truly becomes an issue that prevents sharing, one possible solution is to intentionally group those of similar status in the smaller groups if possible and appropriate. While these group encounters cannot do away with the realities of asymmetric power relationships that may exist "outside of the group," facilitators can assure participants that relationships are equalitarian within the group context of the Story Circle experience (meaning that no one participant has more rights than others and that all are granted equal respect).

7) Debriefing can also be a challenge, depending on the group participants (for example, debriefing in a language other than their first language). To facilitate debriefing in such cases, it may be helpful to have participants spend time writing their reflections first before being asked to share (by using the worksheet at the end of this Manual), to combine two smaller groups together and debrief in this way instead of as a whole larger group, or use selected photos and other visual mechanisms for debriefing that don't necessarily involve sharing one's thoughts verbally with the group. (See the section on adapting Story Circles for other ideas on this.)

8) Another challenge for Story Circles can be ensuring that there is adequate time for the setup, the actual storytelling/sharing and discussion, and the debrief/discussion. It is very important to never skip or shorten the debriefing time, as this is a key part of the tool since it involves

the crucial reflection elements in developing intercultural competencies. While it may be acceptable to provide time parameters for the actual sharing of the stories (even 3–5 minutes per person, for example), it is imperative that adequate time be allotted for implementing the tool in its entirety (usually a minimum of 90 minutes, depending on the number of participants, although 120+ minutes is preferable).

There may be other challenges encountered, including personality (such as shyness) or influences from one's cultural background (see further sections in the manual for some possible intercultural issues that could arise during the sharing of personal experiences). It is important for facilitators to think through some possible challenges that may occur, such as the ones outlined here, and others that may be unique to particular contexts and situations, and have a plan for addressing them.

Follow-up from a Story Circle experience

Facilitators, or others involved, may want to follow-up with the participants after the Story Circle experience, especially since the purpose in this case is individuals' continued development of intercultural competencies, which is a lifelong process. Follow-up could involve using other tools such as the participant's action plan (found at the end of this manual) or the autobiography of intercultural encounters (see the section in this manual about additional tools). It may be helpful to engage participants in reflective one-on-one conversations as to how they felt they had enhanced their own intercultural competencies development and their plans for continuing to work on various elements of intercultural competencies (what specifically they want to focus on – i.e., understanding other perspectives, openness, empathy, and how they specifically plan to develop these elements more within themselves).

It would also be helpful if facilitators encouraged participants to maintain contact with each other (if appropriate) in order to continue building relationships with each other and further developing their intercultural competencies. To that end, it would be good, if time permits, to discuss with the whole group ways to continue follow-up on the initial Story Circle experience as well as expectations for follow-up. For example, some participants may be expecting to continue to develop the relationships that were started within the circles and others may not have those same expectations. This mismatch in expectations regarding follow-up could lead not only to disappointment but also to disillusionment, which could prove to be a setback in developing intercultural competencies. Thus it is important to take the follow-up from Story Circles quite seriously and, at a minimum, discuss this further with participants.

Photo 2.5 Story Circles pilot in Tunis, Tunisia
Source: ©UNESCO/IADH

Box 2.5   Using Story Circles for boosting youth creativity and self-awareness in Tunisia

The implementation of the Story Circles in Tunisia was a great achievement, with very interested and actively engaged participants attending the sessions with enthusiasm and diligence until the last moment. This pilot notably encouraged these young women and men to engage in other activities (workshops, seminars, etc.) as part of their associative commitment.

The pilot session enabled the adaptation of a global approach to a particular Tunisian context promoting the following:

- A spirit of cooperation and openness between young people to share their personal and intimate experiences, especially with other young people who are not necessarily in their closer group of friends. Participants immediately developed skills, such as empathy and mutual respect.
- Young people's creativity through self-awareness and engagement with other people, close communities, and the world. This activity allowed young Tunisians from different regions, ages, and social classes to communicate, listen, and express themselves

with confidence. We experienced very powerful moments, such as the presentation of a poem and the improvisation of a rap.

- Capacity building of new facilitators. Very attentive to the methodology, as well as to the instructions, they adapted the guide to the local context, being very sensitive to the differences of age, gender, and the social dimension.

As a facilitator, I noticed that the participants followed the principles of the methodology across all the exercises of the session. They began to rethink their relationships with others through intercultural communication. The difference was also no longer a problem for them as they turned their diversity into positive assets.

The self-confidence, openness, and very positive engagement of these young people were remarkable – which can be illustrated by their interest in contacting facilitators and sharing very positive messages about the piloting session.

I believe that the success of this methodology in the Tunisian pilot experience was due to several factors: 1) its relevance, adaptability, and flexibility; 2) the importance of the main subject, which concerns the whole of humanity; 3) the wish of young participants to put their stamp in this important guide, which should be a reference for the Arab region; 4) the efforts made by the organizers (UNESCO and the Arab Institute for Human Rights); and 5) the commitment of the facilitators and the enthusiasm of the young people.

To carry out the implementation of this guide, especially in the Middle East and North Africa region, it is recommended to

- strengthen the capacity of facilitators to better explain the methodology and bring out creativity among young people;
- support training of young facilitators because of their role as influencers among other young women and men;
- use creative arts methods, including drama, dance, and body language activities;
- contextualize the methodology for the three major Arab regions: the Gulf countries, the Middle East, and the Great Arab Maghreb (North Africa); and
- promote this guide as a pedagogical tool for more inclusive and effective education.

Kheireddini Abdelli – trainer of a Tunisian NGO

As a trainee for the Arab Institute for Human Rights and a mentor in the leadership-building project "Building Youth Resilience in Tunisia and the Netherlands," I have found the Story Circles to be a crucial tool in supporting support my work to address communication issues among youth. Throughout my professional experience, I have been able to notice weak communication among Tunisian youth, based either on a lack of skills or an absence of interest in getting to know others.

The pilot session of the UNESCO Manual on Intercultural Competencies in Tunis was an opportunity for me to get a broader view of intercultural competencies, as well as to become familiar with the Story Circles methodology. Around 20 teenagers, aged 15–20 years old, from different areas of Tunis participated in the pilot session. The Tunisian community is diverse in the sense that young people have a different set of values and different visions of the future. Our community is not based on several languages, religions, or nationalities, but on different mind-sets.

At the beginning, the young women and men were eager to know more about the workshop. My colleague and I started to explain the rules of the process and divided the group into two subgroups of five members to create a more intimate space. When I started to set the time for each activity, the teenagers said that they did not need it because they had nothing to say to each other. I tried to encourage them to listen respectfully, highlighting that Story Circles are not just about storytelling, rather they are about the interaction with the other.

At the end of the session, they were surprised how well they were able to describe each other after listening to the stories – even if in the debriefing they noted that time was insufficient for the activity. At the same time, they declared that they did not expect the session would be so active, interesting, and useful. The majority of them have previous experience in social work within local NGOs and expressed appreciation for the training, highlighting that Story Circles could be helpful in improving their engagement with other youth. They also declared that the Story Circles empowered them to listen, although they had never considered them as an important tool for communication.

This training gave space for human interaction, building relationships, and – most importantly – empowering young leaders with different backgrounds to use the methodology of Story Circles. What they have experienced allowed them to adopt a new vision toward others and to have faith in what they are doing. Some of the teenagers expressed that the training has given them something to look forward, as it has changed their interpretations of the present and their visions toward the future of their communities. They also promised that they would share the experience with young women and men that they are working with or with whom they interact.

Being able to see the light at the end of the tunnel can push young people to bring up all their efforts to achieve their goals. Within this workshop, I was impressed by the potential of youth to stand up for their communities and realize the importance of what they can do either at the local or national levels. They were able to set their minds free from negativity, passivity, and unresponsiveness toward the other.

Yasmine Wartani – trainee of the Arab
Institute for Human Rights*

*The Arab Institute for Human Rights is an independent Arab NGO founded in 1989 and based in Tunisia. The institute aims to promote a culture of human rights in the Arab region, as enshrined in the Universal Declaration of Human Rights and international conventions, through developing human rights education methodologies and tools, organizing capacity-building programs, and participating in the institutions and public policies reforms by using the human rights–based approach

----

The problem is with us and not black magic spells or curses.
Integrity ennobles us and makes us forget our deficiencies.
Unity improves us and our differences enhance us.
Woe is me, woe is you and woe to the elephant that tramples!
In trying to eradicate difference, we extinguish all brilliance and light
(. . .)
We shall vanquish our division and reject our fragmentation.
We shall restore our dignity and righteousness.
We shall rescue our people from the depths of our injustice;
We shall send forth the torch of light into to every dark place that
    troubles us.
Then I shall remind you: My people, I am just like you.

Extract from the poem by Ms. Briki Islem proclaimed on the occasion of the pilot of the Manual on Intercultural Competencies in Tunisia

Criteria and preparation of facilitators

Criteria for Story Circle facilitators include those who have a welcoming presence (meaning that they are approachable and calming), who are comfortable in front of a group, who are familiar with the context and backgrounds of the Story Circle participants (including awareness of cultural norms and expectations of the participants and of the culture in which the tool is being used), who are appropriate for the particular context, and who can thoughtfully guide group discussion, including *listening for understanding*. It is important for facilitators to be authentic and able to relate well to those from different backgrounds. Furthermore, the welcome and opening comments are key in framing the Story Circle experience appropriately and in ensuring that the experience is a positive one for all participants. Therefore, it may be wise for facilitators to spend adequate time in preparing for the Story Circle experience, especially in framing and setting up the experience in the beginning with participants. (See the criteria list at the end of the manual for more on this, including intercultural facilitation competencies.)

Preparation for Story Circles facilitators need not involve formal intercultural training, although it is best for Story Circle facilitators to have had some intercultural training and at a minimum general facilitation experience in working with groups. The best way to learn about facilitating a Story Circle is to participate in one first, and if none exist, then organizing a Story Circle is a good way to start. To prepare for the role of facilitator, a person needs to be thoroughly familiar with the material in this manual and ideally read at least one or more of the recommended readings in the resource list. In addition, it may be helpful to "test" the tool with a smaller group of people (since the best preparation is facilitating a Story Circle) before using it with a larger group of people.

Note: To facilitate more in-depth Story Circles that have the potential of delving into intercultural conflict situations or intensely emotional situations, it is highly recommended to have a trained facilitator skilled at navigating emotions and conflict (although given that the purpose of these Story Circles is to develop intercultural competencies, exploring intercultural conflict should not be the goal or included in any of the specific prompts). In this case, however, a background in intercultural conflict resolution may be desirable, as well as some knowledge of intercultural theories and concepts (see resource list). Again, however, the facilitator can determine the degree of depth by selecting appropriate prompts that will be used, which should align with the overall goal of individuals' intercultural competencies development.

Preferably, there would be two facilitators per Story Circle as co-facilitators. This is helpful to model diversity (i.e., one male and one female, different ages, or two from different backgrounds) as well as having one person available to work one-on-one with someone in case emotions become overwhelming or other issues arise.

Intercultural tips for facilitators include the following:

- Communicate clearly by using simple language, paraphrasing, and rephrasing instructions.
- Refrain from asking yes/no questions.
- Refrain from calling on individuals specifically.
- Interpret communication and behavior (including nonverbal and what is *not* said) of participants in multiple ways.
- Be patient.
- Be very aware of how and what you are as the facilitator.
- Be very aware of the behaviors of your participants (observe and listen carefully) and try to understand those behaviors through the eyes of your participants, resisting judging them or interpreting such behaviors through your lens.
- Display cultural humility, meaning that you model a "willing and curious to learn" attitude that demonstrates that the facilitator's way of seeing the world is just one viewpoint (versus a "know-it-all" attitude of someone having "all the answers").

Additional intercultural training tips for facilitators

For those interested in engaging in further intercultural competencies development with participants beyond the use of Story Circles, and in utilizing additional intercultural tools (such as those found in books at the end of this manual), it is important to remember the following:

a) Develop clear and realistic goals around intercultural competencies development, remembering that participants are at different stages in their own intercultural development.
b) Meet participants where they are (find out what their needs and questions are) and ensure that the intercultural training (including content and activities) is relevant to participants (meaning that it meets their needs).
c) Create an appropriate and safe learning environment (see tips for creating a safe environment at the end of this manual), matching the training and learning activities with the stated training goals.
d) Recognize that a one-time intercultural training is usually insufficient for achieving the training goals (particularly regarding intercultural competencies development) and ideally, needs to include several iterations of intercultural training over time.

(For more on designing and implementing intercultural competencies training, see Gregersen-Hermans & Pusch, 2012).

Box 2.6   Piloting intercultural competencies in Istanbul with the Aladdin Project*

The Aladdin Project's International University for Intercultural Leadership (IUIL) is an annual two-week course that brings together students from 53 partner universities on five continents. It is supported by UNESCO and has received funding from the European Commission's Erasmus Plus program. Sixty to 70 students from Europe, the Middle East, Asia, Africa, and the Americas attend the two-week program to attain intercultural skills and study key issues in international affairs that are linked to coexistence, diversity, the rule of law, and good governance.

During the 2018 edition of the IUIL, a rapid Story Circle exercise was undertaken with 60 participating students who were introduced to the background and rationale behind the methodology and the growing evidence of the importance of intercultural competencies. Indeed, today there is broad recognition of the importance of intercultural competencies for promoting cultural awareness and respectful interactions, thus building capacities to prevent and peacefully manage the rise of ethno-cultural conflicts. Linkages between intercultural competencies, employability, and economic competitiveness have also been identified, and these same competencies can create awareness of pressing global issues, along with the desire to play a role in tackling related challenges.

Although this pilot was far shorter than a normal exercise, the students quickly grasped the objectives, principles, and guidelines for the methodology, and engaged with enthusiasm in an intensive simulation, which led to very useful recommendations, such as 1) stressing the importance of maintaining "equality" in the group as the storytelling moves on, hence the need for accountability and robust means of reaching mutual understanding throughout; 2) the necessity of leaving more space for feelings/emotions during the exercise in addition to "*listening for understanding*," which is powerful but insufficient; and 3) the introduction of free and self-defined options on intercultural themes and the identification of a neutral way of deciding on "who starts" in a given Story Circle.

The presence of students from diverse backgrounds, including some from conflict zones or countries or regions in conflict or dispute – such as Israeli and Palestinian, Turkish and Kurdish, Syrian, and Lebanese students – made the exercise extremely concrete. Some sensitive issues emerged. The widely shared perception among students from African and Arab countries, for example, was that Western students were always given greater space and opportunity to express their views and narratives, and some felt that uneven language skills put them at a disadvantage. Another important issue was the importance of developing empathy, primarily by training oneself to listen with total concentration to the others and absorb and process their accounts rather than follow one's trail of thought and ideas.

An intercultural competencies "Story Circle" exercise for students will be included in future editions of the Aladdin Project's International Summer University.

Sacha Silbermann Apeloig – staff, Aladdin Project

. . . .

*The Aladdin Project is an independent, international NGO based in Paris. Aladdin's founders were initially inspired by the need to counter the falsification of history in the shape of Holocaust denial and trivialization. The project is based on the idea that lasting intercultural dialogue can only thrive in an interchange that is at peace with history.

Possible intercultural communication issues

Communication, even through storytelling and personal sharing, is hard work, so it is good to explore what blocks people from truly communicating with each other. Often, what was meant is not what was understood (since stories and communication are interpreted through another's lens, which may be composed of age, gender, culture, socio-economic class, religion, race, and so on), so **checking for clarity is important** (this may mean asking questions to seek better understanding of what was shared – *after* the stories have all been shared or using the phrase "help me understand more about . . . ."). Then there is also the **issue of language**, especially since language is often quite culturally situated with use of idiomatic expressions, cultural references, and so on, which may make it difficult to understand the other, even when presumably speaking the same language. It is helpful to remind participants to **speak clearly and simply**. Other issues when communicating across cultural differences can also include the **level of detail** and specificity given, whether a meaning is **implied or directly stated**, and the **degree of formality** one uses depending on the perceived social role and status of individuals. Sometimes it can be helpful to look for what was *not* said, since that may actually be the message. So, not relying only on words is important when communicating since much of communication occurs beyond the actual words that are said. Emotion, stress, and conflict (as well as physical factors, such as fatigue or hunger) can heighten existing communication issues and lead to further misunderstandings. For more on intercultural communication, see the resources listed at the end of this manual.

To address intercultural communication issues that may arise, some basic caveats should be observed (and even stated at the beginning of a Story Circle experience during the development of group guidelines):

1) **Respect self and others.**
2) **Avoid making assumptions, although that's quite natural as humans to do.**[3]
3) **Don't take personal offense at what or how something is said.**
4) **Refrain from judgmental or critical comments.**
5) **Presume positive intent.**
6) **Speak only from personal experience and not on behalf of others.**
7) **Maintain curiosity.**

Addressing some of these intercultural issues may be helpful in either the debriefing portion of the Story Circles or possibly in the setup in the beginning, depending on what is most appropriate for the context and participants. At a minimum, it is important for Story Circle facilitators to be aware of and anticipate such intercultural issues during the implementation of Story Circles.

Suggestions for adapting Story Circles

There are many ways that Story Circles can be adapted, based on the context and group, including the following:

Prompts: One of the main ways to adapt story circles to specific groups or contexts is in developing a specific intercultural prompt for use in that particular setting. The ones suggested here are more generic in nature and can be used in a wide variety of settings for developing participants' intercultural competencies. However, if in a healthcare setting, for example, the substantive prompt could be more specific, such as, "Tell us about a memorable time when you interacted with a patient who was very different from you and what you learned about yourself and the other person." See materials at the end of this manual for criteria in developing or adapting intercultural prompts.

Physical space: While generally Story Circles take place with participants seated in a circle of chairs, this can also be done standing up in a circle (especially if there are space limitations). It can even be done as a walking Story Circle in which participants actually walk and share (in triads). Walking Story Circles may be more comfortable for some participants instead of being in a formal room. It is important that the space configuration ensures that all participants in the small groups are seen as equal (so the circle is preferred if possible).

Format: The facilitator may wish to have Story Circles be part of a larger workshop or program, which may include an introductory intercultural activity at the beginning (to focus participants on the purpose – see p. 87 for a possible introductory activity) before launching into Story Circles and may incorporate special musical performances, and so on, depending on context.

Group size: Generally, it is recommended to divide into smaller groups of 5–6 for the storytelling portion of the activity so that participants feel more comfortable sharing with a smaller number of people and so that it maximizes the time each person has to share (ideally no fewer than four and no more than seven per group). However, depending on the context, it may be appropriate to share in a larger group of 8–12.

Medium: It is ideal for participants to be face-to-face when sharing their stories. However, there may be times when this can be done via technology (such as Skype or FaceTime). In some situations, it may be appropriate to share pre-recorded stories via video, although this would not allow for real-time sharing. In the case of video, the debriefing and discussion afterward, as well as intentional follow-up, are crucial.

Extending the stories: In some situations, it may be appropriate to encourage participants to share their stories via radio, video, through written articles, or through other creative expressions (art, drama, etc.) so that there can be an even greater impact beyond those who participate in the face-to-face experience. For example, in some countries, such as the United States, this has been done quite successfully in training and empowering participants to then in turn go and lead Story Circles, and even in recording some of them for use on the radio.

Box 2.7   Implementing Story Circles on a small island and developing state – the pilot in Vanuatu

A short pilot of the Story Circles was incorporated in the final day of the Workshop on Education for Sustainable Development, Global Citizenship Education: Preparing Youth for an Inclusive, Peaceful, and Sustainable Society, that was held in November 2018 in Port Vila, Vanuatu – a small island and developing state.

All participants were representatives of either national youth councils or provincial youth councils. Most of them had very little experience with communication in a multicultural context.

The activity was included in the last day of the workshop, which has allowed all participants to be familiar with each other (at a certain level) and has prevented any introduction among participants at the start of the Story Circles session.

As some participants from outer islands in Vanuatu were not comfortable with speaking in English, the group discussion was mostly conducted in Bislama. The use of the mother language was critical to ensure that the facilitators, as well as participants, understood the meaning of the questions and the methodology.

The Story Circles activity bears indeed significant resemblance to the concept of "talanoa" – a methodology often associated with community gathering and storytelling in communal spaces – in the Pacific, including among Melanesian countries. Therefore, a few participants referred to the activity as "talanoa." The major difference is that in the talanoa approach, the role of the facilitator gravitates more toward leadership, which allows the facilitator to direct the flow of the discussion. At the same time, seniority is a key player in "talanoa" when the hierarchy might allow senior members more speaking time and space for giving comment and feedback to others.

Both of these parameters came into play during the Story Circles session. While half of the facilitators were rather junior, they had difficulty controlling the discussion during the debriefing round when there was the presence of more senior members in the group.

In this regard, the use of a "talking piece" was reported by all facilitators as very helpful, especially when there were members in the group who seemed to dominate the discussion. The talking piece was a more "polite way" to ensure the principle of equal opportunity among all – especially in the group composed by some senior members.

Harry James Olikwailafa – president
of the Honiara Youth Council

Additional reflection tools

Depending on the group, context, and situation, facilitators may want to delve further into intercultural explorations based on the initial Story Circles sharing in order to further develop participants' intercultural competencies.

Reflection tools can be transformational in encouraging participants to think more deeply about themselves and their experiences. The following are some sample specific reflection tools that can be used to further develop participants' intercultural competencies and engage them in thinking interculturally.

What? So what? Now what?

Use these three questions to move beyond describing what was learned, although that becomes the starting point. Specifically, ask the following:

a)   What? What did I learn from this experience (about myself, about others, about navigating differences?)
b)   So what? Why is this learning important?
c)   Now what? What will I do now as a result of this learning?

I used to think . . . now I think . . . (Ritchhart et al., 2011)

This reflection tool demonstrates the change that can occur from an experience, whether it is a change in knowledge or attitude or skill. This reflection prompt can be adapted to include other areas, such as "*I used to know . . . now I know . . .*" or "*Earlier I couldn't . . . now I can . . .*" And so on. It is important for the facilitator to note that there is no right or wrong answers, and that this is simply about being open to the new insights and learning that emerged from the experience.

3Cs (adapted from Ritchhart et al., 2011)

After listening to the stories, the following can be explored further:

Connections: What connections are there between the stories you heard and your own experiences?
Concepts: What key ideas or insights emerged from the stories that are important and need further reflection?
Changes: What changes or adjustments in attitudes, thoughts, or actions are needed in order to navigate differences better in the future?

These questions can be answered through discussion or through visual depictions, such as a collage.

OSEE (Deardorff, 2012)

This OSEE tool helps participants move beyond making assumptions.

O – Observe and listen carefully to what is being said

S – State objectively what you hear

E – Explore explanations for the behavior/communication that you observed (explanations could include cultural, physical, personality, family-related explanations)

E – Evaluate the explanations as to which one or ones is the most likely for the observed behavior/communication

Autobiography of intercultural encounters (adapted from Council of Europe)

This tool is designed to help analyze a specific intercultural encounter through a series of questions. The focus is on one encounter – in this case the Story Circles experience – with one particular person from a different cultural background (in this case, one person within the Story Circle could be referenced or the experience itself could be referenced in the reflection). The first question starts with self-definition. Other questions address the basics of the experience – what happened, when, where, and so on. The questions then go deeper into the personal reflection (note that these have been adapted to the Story Circle experience but could be used in other intercultural encounters):

*What surprised you?

*Why did you choose to participate in this Story Circle experience?

*What did you learn about yourself?

- What were your feelings during this encounter/experience?
- How would you describe the others' feelings during this encounter/experience?
- What could you have done differently in this experience in terms of listening, understanding, and adjusting to each other?
- How were your actions/thoughts influenced by an idea you had about the other?
- What are you curious about now and want to learn more about?
- How do you feel you have grown or changed through the experience?
- What do you know now that you didn't know before (about yourself and about others in your Story Circle)?
- What do you understand only after reflecting on the experience?

Conclusion

Following the overview of some intercultural tools and approaches, this manual puts forth Story Circles as a key tool for developing individuals' intercultural competencies, in particular aspects of cultural self-awareness, listening, respect, other awareness, and empathy with reflection at the core. This is a tool that gives participants the opportunity to actually practice intercultural competencies (especially *listening for understanding*) and can be adapted to many different groups and contexts around the world. This manual also includes an extensive resource list that includes books on specific intercultural training tools; books that can help prepare facilitators of Story Circles, as well as those desiring to learn more about intercultural theory and knowledge, and websites of additional intercultural resources. The manual ends with practical handouts and other materials for use by facilitators in leading Story Circles.

In conclusion, it is critically important to offer "efficient quality, formal and non-formal learning opportunities for everyone to acquire the intercultural competencies required for successful living in the modern complexity of our heterogeneous world" (UNESCO, 2013a, pp. 38–39). Story Circles provides an example of an experiential learning methodology that connects participants while honing intercultural competencies. As a tool, Story Circles can be adapted and used in not only developing intercultural competencies in individuals but also in bridging divides and in furthering intercultural dialogue and understanding which are so vital in today's world as we learn to live together.

Theoretical basis for Story Circles in developing intercultural competencies (further detail and explanation can be found in the references listed next):

Intercultural competence model (Figure 2.1)

From "The Identification and Assessment of Intercultural Competence as a Student Outcome of Internationalization at Institutions of Higher Education in the United States" by Dr. Darla K. Deardorff in Journal of Studies in International Education, Fall 2006, 10, p. 241–266 and in *The SAGE Handbook of Intercultural Competence*, 2009 (Thousand Oaks: Sage)

Process Model of Intercultural Competence (Deardorff, 2006, 2009, 2012):

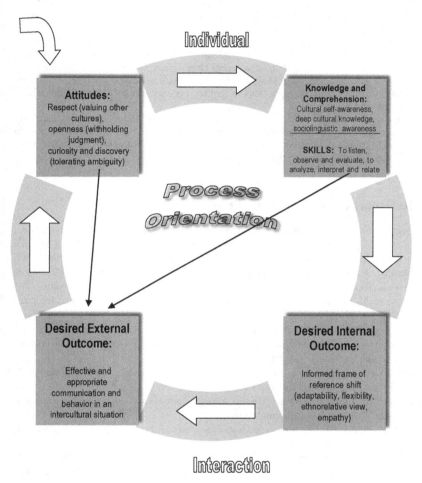

Figure 2.1 Intercultural competence model

Source: Dr. Darla K. Deardorff in *Journal of Studies in International Education*, Fall 2006, 10, p. 241–266 and in *The SAGE Handbook of Intercultural Competence*, 2009 (Thousand Oaks: Sage)

Notes:

- *Begin with attitudes. Move from the individual level (attitudes) to the interaction level (outcomes).*
- *Degree of intercultural competence depends on acquired degree of attitudes, knowledge/ comprehension, and skills.*

Copyright 2006 by D. K. Deardorff

Notes

1 Transformational here means that one is able to gain new perspectives as well as learn to listen for understanding instead of listening for response or judgment, which is most often the case.
2 The meaning of "equality" may need to be discussed within the group first since there may not be a shared understanding of what is meant by "equality," which is critical for the Story Circle to work. Here "equality" means having the same rights within the space of the Story Circle, as well as having the same status and role within the circle, regardless of gender, age, social class, educational attainment, and so on.
3 To avoid making assumptions, it is important to listen and observe very carefully first and then to consider different explanations for the communication issue at hand – this can often start by asking, "Help me understand why. . . ." See additional tools for more on the OSEE tool.

References and further readings

Arévalo-Guerrero, E. (2009). *Assessing the development of learners' intercultural sensitivity and intercultural communicative competence: The intercultural Spanish course* (Unpublished doctoral dissertation). College Park: University of Maryland.

Bennett, J. (2012). The developing art of intercultural facilitation. In K. Berardo & D. K. Deardorff (Eds.), *Building cultural competence.* Sterling, VA: Stylus.

Bennett, M. (1993). Towards ethnorelativism: A developmental model of intercultural sensitivity (revised). In R. M. Paige (Ed.), *Education for the intercultural experience.* Yarmouth, ME: Intercultural Press.

Berardo, K., & Deardorff, D. K. (2012). *Building cultural competence: Innovative activities and models.* Sterling, VA: Stylus.

Brown, B. (2012). *Daring greatly: How the courage to be vulnerable transforms the way we live, love, parent, and lead.* New York: Avery.

Byram, M. (1997). *Teaching and assessing intercultural communicative competence.* Clevedon: Multilingual Matters.

Chaitlin, J. (2003). *Creating safe spaces for communication.* Retrieved from www.beyondintractability.org/essay/safe-spaces

Council of Europe. (2009). *Autobiography of intercultural encounters.* Strasbourg: Council of Europe Publishing. Retrieved from www.coe.int/t/dg4/autobiography/default_en.asp

Council of Europe. (2015). *TASKs for democracy: 60 activities to learn and assess transversal attitudes, skills, and knowledge.* Strasbourg: Council of Europe.

Deardorff, D. K. (2009). Synthesizing conceptualizations of intercultural competence. In D. K. Deardorff (Ed.), *The Sage handbook of intercultural competence.* Thousand Oaks: Sage.

Deardorff, D. K. (2012). OSEE tool. In K. Berardo & D. K. Deardorff (Eds.), *Building cultural competence: Innovative activities and models.* Sterling: Stylus.

Denning, S. (2005). *The leader's guide to storytelling.* San Francisco: Jossey-Bass.

Donders, Y., & Laaksonen, A. (2014). *Taking a human rights-based approach to intercultural competencies.* Paris: UNESCO.

DuBois, R., & Li, M. (1963). *The art of group conversation: A new breakthrough in social communication.* New York: National Board of Young Men's Christian Associations.

Gregersen-Hermans, J., & Pusch, M. (2012). How to design and assess an intercultural learning experience. In K. Berardo & D. K. Deardorff (Eds.), *Building cultural competence.* Sterling: Stylus.

Gudykunst, W. (2005). *Theorizing about intercultural communication.* Thousand Oaks: Sage.

Hall, E. T. (1981). *Beyond culture.* New York, NY: Doubleday.

Hall, M., Ainsworth, K., & Telling, S. (2012). *Training and assessment in intercultural competence: A critical review of contemporary practice in business education.* Aston Business School. Retrieved from www.heacademy.ac.uk/system/files/ aston_interculturalcompetence_criticalreview.pdf

Haven, K. (2007). *Story proof: The science behind the startling power of story.* Libraries Unlimited.

Haven, K. (2014). *Story smart: Using the science of story to influence, persuade, inspire and teach.* Libraries Unlimited.

Hofstede, G. (2001). *Culture's consequences: Comparing values, behaviors, institutions and organizations across nations* (2nd ed.). Thousand Oaks: Sage.

Holliday, A., Hyde, M., & Kullman, J. (2010). *Intercultural communication: An advanced resource book for students.* New York: Routledge.

IEREST. (2015). *Intercultural education resources for Erasmus students and their teachers.* Koper: Annales University Press.

Kim, Y. Y. (2009). The identity factor in intercultural competence. In D. K. Deardorff (Ed.), *The Sage handbook of intercultural competence.* Thousand Oaks: Sage.

King, P. M., & Baxter-Magolda, M. B. (2005). A developmental model of intercultural maturity. *Journal of College Student Development, 46*(6), 571–592.

Mezirow, J. (1990). How critical reflection triggers transformative learning. *Fostering Critical Reflection in Adulthood,* 1–20. San Francisco: Jossey-Bass.

Nwosu, P. (2009). Understanding Africans' conceptualizations of intercultural competence. In D. K. Deardorff (Ed.), *The Sage handbook of intercultural competence.* Thousand Oaks: Sage.

Pranis, K. (2005). *The little book of circle processes.* Pennsylvania: Good Books.

Ritchhart, R., Church, M., & Morrison, K. (2011). *Making thinking visible: How to promote engagement, understanding, and independence for all learners.* San Francisco: Jossey-Bass.

Shirts, G. (1977). *BaFa BaFa: A cross-cultural simulation game.* Del Mar, CA: Simile Two.

Siblot, P. (1997). *Defining tolerance.* Paris: UNESCO.

Spitzberg, B., & Changon, G. (2009). Conceptualizing intercultural competence. In D. K. Deardorff (Ed.), *The Sage handbook of intercultural competence* (pp. 2–52). Thousand Oaks: Sage.

Stringer, D. M., & Cassiday, P. A. (2009). *52 activities for improving cross-cultural communication.* Yarmouth, ME: Intercultural Press.

Thiagarajan, S., & Thiagarajan, R. (2011). *Barnga: A simulation game on cultural clashes: 25th anniversary edition.* London: Nicholas Brealey.

Ting-Toomey, S. (1999). *Communicating across cultures.* New York, NY: Guilford.

Triandis, H. (1979). *Handbook of cross-cultural psychology*. Allyn & Bacon.

UNESCO. (1996). *Learning: The treasure within: Report to UNESCO of the international commission on education for the twenty-first century (highlights)*. Paris: UNESCO.

UNESCO. (2001). *UNESCO Universal Declaration on Cultural Diversity*. Paris: UNESCO.

UNESCO. (2013a). *UNESCO's programme of action: Culture of peace and non-violence*. Paris: UNESCO.

UNESCO. (2013b). *Intercultural competencies: Conceptual and operational framework*. Paris: UNESCO.

UNESCO. (2015). *Global citizenship education: Topics and learning objectives*. Paris: UNESCO.

UNESCO. (2017). *Education for sustainable development goals: Learning objectives*. Paris: UNESCO.

UNESCO. (2018). *Global citizenship education: Taking it local*. Paris: UNESCO.

Wang, Y., Deardorff, D. K., & Kulich, S. (2017). Intercultural competence in international higher education: A Chinese perspective. In D. K. Deardorff & L. Arasaratnam-Smith (Eds.), *Intercultural competence in higher education: International approaches, assessment and application*. London: Routledge.

Zwicky, C. (2005). The circle process in schools. In K. Pranis (Ed.), *The little book of circle processes* (pp. 71–73). Pennsylvania: Good Books.

Recommended readings in preparing to facilitate Story Circles for intercultural competencies development

Bennett, J. (2012). The developing art of intercultural facilitation. In K. Berardo & D. K. Deardorff (Eds.), *Building cultural competence*. Sterling, VA: Stylus. Retrieved from https://sty.presswarehouse.com/sites/stylus/resrcs/chapters/1579228046_otherchap.pdf

Bennett, M. (1998). Intercultural communication: A current perspective. In M. J. Bennett (Ed.), *Basic concepts of intercultural communication: Selected readings*. Yarmouth, ME: Intercultural Press. Retrieved from www.mairstudents.info/intercultural_communication.pdf

Deardorff, D. K. (n.d.). *Theory reflections: Intercultural competence framework*. Retrieved from www.nafsa.org/_/File/_/theory_connections_intercultural_competence.pdf

Leeds-Hurwitz, W. (2014). *Intercultural communication*. Retrieved from https://centerforinterculturaldialogue.files.wordpress.com/2014/03/key-concept-intercultural-comm.pdf

UNESCO. (2013). *Intercultural competencies: Conceptual and operational framework*. Paris: UNESCO. Retrieved from http://unesdoc.unesco.org/images/0021/002197/219768e.pdf

Practical resources for intercultural competencies development

This resource list includes a sampling of books on specific intercultural training tools; books that can help prepare facilitators of Story Circles, as well as those desiring to learn more about intercultural theory and knowledge; and websites of additional intercultural resources. To date, the resources included here are those primarily available in English. However, it is important to recognize that there are many other intercultural resources available in many different languages other than English. Thus this list serves as a starting point only and is a work in progress as intercultural resources continue to be added and developed in many languages around the world (see ICC Global website, listed next, for additional resources, including non-English resources).

Berardo, K., & Deardorff, D. K. (2012). *Building cultural competence: Innovative activities and models*. Sterling, VA: Stylus.

Council of Europe. (2015). *TASKs for democracy: 60 activities to learn and assess transversal attitudes, skills, and knowledge*. Strasbourg: Council of Europe.

Fantini, A. E. (1997). *New ways in teaching culture*. Alexandria, VA: TESOL.

Fowler, S., & Mumford, M. (Eds.). (1995/1999). *Intercultural sourcebook: Cross-cultural training methods* (Vols. 1 & 2). Yarmouth, ME: Intercultural Press.

Hughes, G., & Thiagarajan, S. (2013). *Photo Jolts! Image-based activities that increase clarity, creativity, and conversation*. SAH. Amazon.

Kappler-Mikk, B., Cohen, A. D., & Paige, R. M. (2009). *Maximizing study abroad: An instructional guide to strategies for language and culture learning and use*. Minneapolis, MN: Center for Advanced Research on Language Acquisition.

Kohls, L. R., & Knight, J. (1994). *Developing intercultural awareness: A cross-cultural training handbook* (2nd ed.). Yarmouth, ME: Intercultural Press.

Seelye, H. N. (1996). *Experiential activities for intercultural learning*. Yarmouth, ME: Intercultural Press.

Storti, C. (2017). *Cross-cultural dialogues: 74 brief encounters with cultural difference* (2nd ed.). Boston: Intercultural Press.

Stringer, D. M., & Cassiday, P. A. (2003). *52 activities for exploring value differences*. Yarmouth, ME: Intercultural Press.

Stringer, D. M., & Cassiday, P. A. (2009). *52 activities for improving cross-cultural communication*. Yarmouth, ME: Intercultural Press.

Some practical websites on intercultural tools and resources

Autobiography of Intercultural Encounters. Retrieved from www.coe.int/t/dg4/autobiography/default_en.asp

CEFCult Toolkit for Intercultural Communicative Competence Training Materials. Retrieved from http://cefcult.eu/data/CEFcult_toolkit_students_2011-11FIN.pdf

Critical Incidents for Intercultural Communication: An Interactive Tool for Developing Awareness, Knowledge, and Skills. Retrieved from www.norquest.ca/Norquest College/media/pdf/centres/intercultural/CriticalIncidentsBooklet.pdf

ICC Global: Global Network on Intercultural Competence Development. Retrieved from www.iccglobal.org

IEREST Intercultural Education Resources for Erasmus Students and Teachers. Retrieved from www.ierest-project.eu

64   *Story Circles*

Intercultural Communication Bibliography. Retrieved from www.awesomelibrary. org/multicultural-training.html
Intercultural Communication Institute. Retrieved from www.intercultural.org
Intercultural Communication Resource Pack. SALTO Youth. Retrieved from www.salto-youth.net/downloads/4-17-1789/Booklet%20Intercultural%20 Communication%20Resource%20Pack.pdf
Intercultural Training Pack. Retrieved from www.culturewise.net/wp-content/ uploads/2013/05/Cultural-awareness-training-exercise-pack.pdf
NAFSA Intercultural Activity Toolkit. Retrieved from www.nafsa.org/Professional_ Resources/Browse_by_Interest/Internationalizing_Higher_Education/Network_ Resources/Teaching,_Learning,_and_Scholarship/Intercultural_Activity_Toolkit/
Portfolio on Intercultural Competencies Based on Human Rights (UNESCO). Retrieved from http://unesdoc.unesco.org/images/0023/002311/231132m.pdf
UNESCO e-Platform on Intercultural Dialogue. Retrieved from https://en.unesco. org/interculturaldialogue/
What's up with Culture Website, University of Pacific. Retrieved from www2. pacific.edu/sis/culture/

Some publications on intercultural concepts and theories

Asante, M. K., Miike, Y., & Yin, J. (Eds.). (2013). *The global intercultural communication reader* (2nd ed.). London, UK: Routledge.
Baiutti, M. (2016). Rethinking the concept of intercultural conflict: Italian Returnees' attitudes towards others during a cultural conflict. *FLEKS Scandinavian Journal of Intercultural Theory and Practice, 3*(1), 1–18.
Baldwin, J. R., Coleman, R. M., Gonzalez, A., & Shenoy-Packer, S. (2014). *Intercultural communication for everyday life.* Hoboken, NJ: Wiley-Blackwell.
Bennett, M. J. (Ed.). (2013). *Basic concepts of intercultural communication: Paradigms, principles, and practices* (2nd ed.). Boston, MA: Intercultural Press.
Berry, J. W., Phinney, J. S., San, D. S., & Vedder, P. (2012). *Immigrant youth in cultural transition: Acculturation, identity, and adaptation across national contexts.* New York, NY: Taylor and Francis Group.
Byram, M. (1997). *Teaching and assessing intercultural communicative competence.* Clevedon: Multilingual Matters.
Byram, M. (2008). *From foreign language education to education for intercultural citizenship: Essays and reflections.* Clevedon: Multilingual Matters.
Chen, G. M., & Dai, X. (2014). *Intercultural communication competence: Conceptualization and its development in cultural contexts and interactions.* Newcastle Upon Tyne, UK: Cambridge Scholars Publishing.
Cheong, P. H., Martin, J. N., & Macfadyen, L. P. (2012). *New media and intercultural communication: Identity, community and politics.* New York, NY: Peter Lang Publishing.
Churchill, R. P. (2006). *Human rights and global diversity.* Upper Saddle River, NJ: Pearson and Prentice Hall.
Clayton, J. (2002). *One classroom, many worlds.* Portsmouth, NH: Heinemann.

Cooper, P. J., Calloway-Thomas, C., & Simonds, C. J. (2007). *Intercultural communication: A text with readings.* Boston, MA: Pearson and Allyn and Bacon.

Council of Europe. (2012). *Intercultural competence for all: Preparation for living in a heterogeneous world.* Strasburg: Council of Europe.

Council of Europe. (2014). *Developing intercultural competence through education.* Strasburg: Council of Europe.

Council of Europe. (2016). *Competence for democratic culture: Living together as equals in culturally diverse democratic societies.* Strasburg: Council of Europe.

Deardorff, D. K. (2009). *The Sage handbook of intercultural competence.* Thousand Oaks, CA: Sage.

Fennes, H., & Hapgood, K. (1997). *Intercultural learning in the classroom.* London, UK: Cassell.

Fouad, N. A., & Arredondo, P. (2007). *Becoming culturally oriented: Practical advice for psychologists and educators.* Washington, DC: American Psychologists Press.

Gannon, M. J., & Pillai, R. K. (2012). *Understanding global cultures: Metaphorical journeys through 31 nations, clusters of nations, continents, and diversity* (5th ed.). Thousand Oaks, CA: Sage.

González, A., Houston, M., & Chen, V. (2011). *Our voices: Essays in culture, ethnicity, and communication: An intercultural anthology* (5th ed.). New York, NY: Oxford University Press.

Guerrero, L. K., & Hecht, M. (Eds.). (2007). *The nonverbal communication reader: Classic and contemporary readings* (3rd ed.). Prospect Heights, IL: Waveland Press.

Hall, E. T. (1981). *Beyond culture.* New York, NY: Doubleday.

Hecht, M. L. (Ed.). (1998). *Communicating prejudice.* Thousand Oaks, CA: Sage.

Henderson, G., Spigner-Littles, D., & Hall Millhouse, V. (2006). *A practitioner's guide to understanding indigenous and foreign cultures.* Springfield, IL: Charles C. Thomas.

Hofstede, G. J., Pederson, P. B., & Hofstede, G. (2002). *Exploring culture: Exercises, stories and synthetic cultures.* Boston: Intercultural Press.

Holmes, P. (2015). "The cultural stuff around how to talk to people" immigrants' intercultural communication during a pre-employment work-placement. *Language and Intercultural Communication, 15*(1), 109–124.

Holmes, P., & Dervin, F. (2016). The cultural and intercultural dimensions of English as a Lingua Franca. In *Languages for intercultural communication and education* (Vol. 29). Clevedon, UK: Multilingual Matters.

Holmes, P., & O'Neill, G. (2012). Developing and evaluating intercultural competence: Ethnographies of intercultural encounters. *International Journal of Intercultural Relations, 36*(5), 707–718.

Hua, Z. (Ed.). (2011). *The language and intercultural communication reader.* New York, NY: Routledge.

Jackson, J. (2012). *The Routledge handbook of language and intercultural communication.* New York, NY: Routledge.

Jackson, J. (2014). *Introducing language and intercultural communication.* New York, NY: Routledge.

Jandt, F. E. (2015). *An introduction to intercultural communication: Identities in a global community* (8th ed.). Thousand Oaks, CA: Sage.

Kim, U., Yang, K. S., & Hwang, K. K. (Eds.). (2006). *Indigenous and cultural psychology: Understanding people in context.* New York, NY: Springer SBM Publications.

Landis, D., Bennett, J. M., & Bennett, M. J. (Eds.). (2004). *Handbook of intercultural training* (3rd ed.). Thousand Oaks, CA: Sage Publications.

LeBaron, M., & Pillay, V. (2006). *Conflict across cultures: A unique experience bridging differences.* Boston, MA: Nicholas Brealey.

Lederach, J. P. (2002). *A handbook of international peacebuilding: Into the eye of the storm.* San Francisco, CA: Jossey-Bass.

Lederach, J. P. (2011). *Building peace: Sustainable reconciliation in divided societies.* Washington, DC: United States Institute of Peace.

Leeds-Hurwitz, W. (1993). *Semiotics and communication: Signs, codes, cultures.* Abingdon, UK: Routledge.

Lustig, M. W., & Koester, J. (2012). *Intercultural competence: Interpersonal communication across cultures* (7th ed.). Upper Saddle River, NJ: Pearson Prentice Hall.

Mansouri, F. (Ed.). (2014). *Interculturalism at the crossroads: Comparative perspectives on concepts, policies and practices.* Paris: UNESCO. (available online).

Martin, J. N., & Nakayama, T. K. (2012). *Intercultural communication in contexts* (6th ed.). Boston, MA: McGraw-Hill.

Martin, J. N., & Nakayama, T. K. (2014). *Experiencing intercultural communication: An introduction* (5th ed.). Boston, MA: McGraw-Hill.

Martin, J. N., Nakayama, T. K., & Flores, L. A. (Eds.). (2002). *Readings in intercultural communication: Experiences and contexts* (2nd ed.). Boston, MA: McGraw-Hill.

Matsumoto, D. (Ed.). (2010). *APA handbook of intercultural communication.* Washington, DC: American Psychological Association.

Molinsky, A. (2013). *Global dexterity: How to adapt your behavior across cultures without losing yourself in the process.* Boston, MA: Harvard Business Review Press.

Neuliep, J. W. (2014). *Intercultural communication: A contextual approach* (6th ed.). Thousand Oaks, CA: Sage.

Oetzel, J. G. (2008). *Intercultural communication: A layered approach.* Boston, MA: Allyn & Bacon.

Orbe, M. P., & Harris, T. M. (2013). *Interracial communication: Theory into practice* (3rd ed.). Belmont, CA: Wadsworth.

Paige, R. M. (Ed.). (1993). *Education for the intercultural experience.* Yarmouth, ME: Intercultural Press.

Paulston, C. B., Kiesling, S. F., & Rangel, E. S. (Eds.). (2012). *The handbook of intercultural discourse and communication.* Malden, MA: Wiley-Blackwell.

Payne, R. K. (2005). *Framework for understanding poverty.* Highlands, TX: Aha! Process.

Pedersen, P., Crethar, H., & Carlson, J. (2008). *Inclusive cultural empathy.* Washington, DC: American Psychological Association.

Peterson, B. (2004). *Cultural intelligence: A guide to working with people from other cultures.* Yarmouth, ME: Nicholas Brealey (Intercultural Press).

Prince, D. W., & Hoppe, M. H. (2007). *Communicating across cultures.* Hoboken, NJ: Pfeiffer.

Rothenberg, P. (2006). *Beyond borders: Thinking critically about global issues.* New York, NY: Worth Publishers.

Samovar, L. A., Porter, R. E., & McDaniel, E. R. (Eds.). (2014). *Intercultural communication: A reader* (14th ed.). Independence, KY: Cengage Learning.

Saphiere, D. H., Mikk, B. K., & DeVries, B. I. (2005). *Communication highwire: Leveraging the power of diverse communication styles.* Yarmouth, ME: Intercultural Press (Nicholas Brealey).

Schaetti, B. F., Ramsey, S. J., & Watanabe, G. C. (2008). *Personal leadership: A methodology of two principles and six practices.* Seattle, WA: Flying Kite Publications.

Shaules, J. (2007). *Deep culture: The hidden challenges of global living.* Buffalo, NY: Multilingual Matters.

Sorrells, K. (2012). *Intercultural communication: Globalization and social justice.* Thousand Oaks, CA: Sage.

Spencer-Oatey, H., & Franklin, P. (2009). *Intercultural interaction: A multidisciplinary approach to intercultural communication.* New York: Palgrave Macmillan.

Sternberg, R. J. (Ed.). (2005). *The psychology of hate.* Washington, DC: American Psychological Association.

Storti, C. (2007). *The art of crossing cultures* (2nd ed.). Yarmouth, ME: Intercultural Press.

Storti, C. (2011). *Figuring foreigners out: A practical guide.* Yarmouth, ME: Nicolas Brealey.

Ting-Toomey, S. (1999). *Communicating across cultures.* New York, NY: Guilford.

Ting-Toomey, S., & Chung, L. C. (2011). *Understanding intercultural communication* (2nd ed.). Cary, NC: Oxford University Press.

Ting-Toomey, S., & Oetzel, J. G. (2001). *Managing intercultural conflict effectively.* Thousand Oaks, CA: Sage.

UNESCO. (2013). *Intercultural competencies.* Paris: UNESCO. (available online).

Ward, C. (2013). *Beyond culture shock.* New York, NY: Routledge.

3 Supporting material

I – UNESCO Story Circles Information Sheet

Story Circles were designed as a practical intercultural tool for developing intercultural competencies that can be used in many settings around the world, that can be used outside of formal instructional settings, and that can be facilitated by those who may not have a strong background in intercultural knowledge. Note: UNESCO has successfully piloted this in Thailand, Zimbabwe, Costa Rica, Austria, Tunisia, Turkey, and Vanuatu. This has also been piloted in China and multiple places in the United States.

Story Circles are an adaptable, practical tool that can be used in many different contexts and situations around the world for developing individuals' intercultural competencies and bridging divides. Intercultural competencies are broadly defined as the competences (knowledge, skills, and attitudes) needed to *improve human interactions across difference, whether within a society (differences due to age, gender, religion, socio-economic status, political affiliation, ethnicity, and so on) or across borders.*

Story Circles are a structured yet adaptable tool that focuses on fundamental elements of intercultural competencies development, including respect, listening, curiosity, self- and other awareness, reflection, sharing, empathy, and relationship building. The key to developing intercultural competencies through Story Circles is in the prompt that is used to elicit the sharing of personal experience. (Over a dozen prompts can be found in the manual written to facilitate the Story Circles.) This tool works for developing intercultural competencies only when used with a thorough debriefing/follow-up discussion with participants.

The number of participants can vary dramatically since small groups of 5 are needed for the activity, so this can range from 5–500+. It is important for the small groups to be as diverse as possible (such as gender, age, different backgrounds). All members in the small group need to be able to speak and understand the same language.

Story Circles can be used in a wide variety of settings, including in schools, communities, international development organizations, religious organizations, and professional trainings (such as in healthcare care, police, and teacher education). Note: Story Circles are *not* an intercultural workshop or training. It is very important that Story Circles be framed as experiences or activities (but not as a workshop or training unless they are indeed used as part of a broader intercultural training).

Please allow approximately 90 minutes *minimum* for Story Circles, although more time allocation is preferable. A *general outline* would include the following:

10–15 minutes	Welcome, introductions, overview
10 minutes	Introduction to Story Circles – why (intercultural competencies development) and instructions (emphasize *listening for understanding*) and review handout
5–10 minutes	Get into small groups (of five to six each)
35–45 minutes	Story Circles in small groups
15 minutes	Whole group debrief and conclusions

Note: Other events can be included around the Story Circles, including starting and/ or ending with a meal or performing arts demonstration.

II – General handout – to be used in small groups

This is the general handout to use in the small groups – please write in the prompts to be used.

A – Story Circles: building intercultural competencies

You are about to engage in a Story Circle experience for <u>the purpose of developing intercultural competencies</u>. The following is some important information for you. Please read this first before you begin.

Story Circle goals related to intercultural competencies development and communicating across difference

- <u>Demonstrate respect</u> for others.
- Practice *<u>listening for understanding</u>*.
- <u>Cultivate curiosity</u> about similarities and differences with others.
- Gain <u>increased cultural self-awareness</u>.
- <u>Develop empathy</u>.
- Engage in <u>critical reflection</u> of one's own intercultural competencies development, as well as on the intercultural experience.
- <u>Develop relationships</u> with culturally different others.

Remember

a) Every person has a personal experience that can be shared.
b) We all have something to learn from others.
c) *Listening for understanding* can be transformational.

Story Circle guidelines include

- maintain confidentiality;
- be yourself;
- speak from your own experience only;
- be genuine and authentic;
- keep the sharing simple, clear, and focused;
- uphold positive intent; and
- be comfortable in your own style (i.e., sit, stand, use gestures).

Story Circle instructions

Overview: Sit in a circle, agree on a nonverbal sign to indicate the end of someone's allotted time, and agree together that you will all adhere to the time parameters. The person to the right of the storyteller is the timekeeper. The person who starts is the person whose birthday is closest to today. Now introduce yourselves using the prompt in step #1, which follows. After introductions (#1), take turns sharing your story (using the prompt in #2) – the others need to listen for understanding and *not* interrupt, ask questions, or make comments. Simply listen. Then the next person tells his or her story until all persons in the circle have told their stories – without interruption or comment. Be sure to listen carefully since you will be asked to share a "flashback" from each story at the end (#3). A "flashback" is something that was memorable for you in the story. Be prepared to share this in 15 seconds or less for each story (this is meant to go quickly!).

1)   Sit in a circle, and in *two minutes or less*, briefly introduce yourself by _____.
     No interruptions, comments, or questions. Just take turns introducing yourselves.
2)   *In three minutes or less,*
     _____
     No interruptions, comments, or questions.
3)   Once all stories have been shared, then engage in the "flashback" time: Go back to the first story, and each person (other than the storyteller) shares a specific memorable part of the other's story (in 15 seconds or less). Then go on to the second story, and so on, until "flashbacks" have been shared for all the stories told.
4)   Once the "flashbacks" have been shared, together discuss some of the following questions in the remaining time. *Please monitor the time so the group can finish at the requested time.*

Discussion questions

1)   What common themes did you hear from the stories?
2)   What surprised you?
3)   What challenged you in the stories you heard?
4)   What did you learn about yourself through this experience?

Excerpted from *Manual for Developing Intercultural Competencies: Story Circles* by Darla K. Deardorff, UNESCO/Routledge 2020.

III – Prompts

A. Story Circles prompts examples
(to be used in the same smaller group)

First "get acquainted" round

The following are examples of prompts; the facilitator would **only use one**. The main goal of this first round is to help participants meet each other, begin to build trust, and begin to feel comfortable sharing with each other interculturally (meaning that they begin to reveal something about their own background with a prompt that is directed more at pleasurable topics, such as food, holidays, and so on). Note that even if participants already know each other, it is still helpful to use a "get acquainted" prompt to build trust within the smaller circles.

1) Please tell us your name and the story about your name. (What does it mean? How did you come to have this name?)
2) Please tell us your name and three words or phrases that describe your background and why those words/phrases are important to you.
3) Please tell us about an object or photo that you brought with you that tells us something about you and your background.
4) What is your favorite holiday or festival, and why is this your favorite?
5) What is a favorite food you would eat growing up, and how does that relate to your background?

Second "intercultural competencies" round

The following are examples of intercultural competencies prompts; the facilitator would **only use one**, although if there is sufficient time to engage in the "flashback" after each prompt plus debrief time, then a second prompt could be used. Note that it is important that the selected prompt be aligned with the desired overall outcome of further intercultural competencies development (see the specific goals listed on p. 20).

1) What is one of the most positive interactions you have had with a person(s) who is different from you, and what made this such a positive experience?
2) What is your earliest memory of difference (when you first learned or realized that you were different from someone else)?
3) What is a memorable experience you have had with a person(s) who is different from you (age, religion, gender, socio-economic, culture, nationality, etc.), and what did you learn about yourself and/or the other person in that experience?

4) What is one of the more challenging interactions you have had with a person(s) from a different background, and what did you learn from this?

5) What is a memorable cultural misunderstanding you have had, and what did you learn from this?

6) Describe someone you know personally or who is known to you (via media, in history, etc.) that you feel can get along well with others, especially those who are different from that person. What is it that helps that person get along with others?

7) Describe a time when you realized you believed in a stereotype (about a group you are part of *or* a group that you are not part of) that was not true? What happened?

8) Describe a leader who seems to relate well to people from many different backgrounds. What are the qualities that you admire in this person and why? Which of these qualities are important for positive interactions with others?

9) What is a metaphor from your own experience that illustrates how a cultural clash can be overcome?

10) Describe a time when you felt supported by a community (of friends, colleagues, family members, neighbors). How would you describe this community in terms of similarities and differences, and how did this community demonstrate support?

Excerpted from *Manual for Developing Intercultural Competencies: Story Circles* by Darla K. Deardorff, UNESCO/Routledge 2020.

B. Criteria for developing/adapting Story Circle intercultural prompts

The purpose of the intercultural prompt used in Story Circles is to have participants reflect on their own personal experiences with those who are different from them and share an experience so that the others in the group can begin to see from a different perspective. To develop or adapt an intercultural prompt for use in the Story Circles, the prompt needs to fit the following parameters:

- It is about one specific incident
- It involves the personal experience of the person
- It is framed as an open-ended question or statement (i.e., "Tell us about a time when you . . . .").
- It involves some sort of *intercultural element*, meaning that the prompt is about cultural differences or similarities, about an interaction with those who are different, or about some kind of relationship that involves similarity or difference. Note here that difference can relate to gender, age, religion, socio-economic background, geographic location, ethnicity, etc.
- It includes an element of "lessons learned" or other reflection element
- It is *appropriate* for the person to share
- It is *appropriate* to this local and cultural context
- It is *relevant* to all participants (this is particularly important to ensure when working with children and youth)

In developing/adapting an intercultural prompt to use, be sure that the prompt is not too general or generic. For example, "Tell us about some difficult challenges in your life" is too general and generic *and* does not involve an explicit intercultural element.

IV – Guidelines for facilitators

A. Debriefing and concluding Story Circles

This is a suggested guide for those new to facilitating Story Circles. Facilitators are welcome to adapt any of parts of this guide as needed and appropriate to the specific context.

Start with asking a couple of questions about the experience itself:

1) What is memorable to you about what you heard? (Possible responses may be "how similar we are," "that we share similar feelings," "how important it is to share (or listen).")
2) What surprised you? (There could be a variety of responses here, depending on the prompts used.)
3) What challenged you in the stories you heard? (Possible responses may be "how hard it was to listen without interrupting or asking questions" or "how difficult it was to share about myself.")

Then move to asking questions related more to intercultural competencies development (remember that the ones marked with * are the most important ones to include):

4) *What did you learn about yourself through this experience? (This refers to the goal of increased cultural self-awareness.)
5) *What common themes did you hear from the stories? (Possible responses to common themes could be about sharing similar emotions or similar roles.)
6) *What do you want to explore further after hearing these stories? What are you curious about or want to learn more about regarding similarities and differences with others (this refers to the goal of cultivating curiosity about similarities and differences with others)? Possible responses may include wanting to learn more about someone else's traditions, wanting to hear more about their individual experiences, or maybe going to visit a place that was mentioned in the story.
7) *How has this experience helped you **practice _listening for understanding_ _(this refers to the listening goal related to developing intercultural competence)? Develop empathy?_**

Then ask "bigger-picture" questions that synthesize the learning from the experience into action:

8) Complete this statement: I used to think . . . now I think . . . (an example may be "I used to think international students just wanted to

stay together, but now I think they just may not know how to make friends in the host culture, so I'll more aware of how I interact with international students and work on building friendships").

9) *Stepping back from the experience itself, what are one to two insights you've gained that will help you relate better to those who are different from you?

10) *What will you do now as a result of this experience? (Possible responses could include wanting to continue building the relationships that have started here by meeting up weekly for tea, asking others about their experiences and trying to listen better for understanding, reading more intercultural articles, facilitating a Story Circle, and so on. This is a good time to mention the action plan that each could develop – see the other handout for an actual action plan template.)

11) *How has this larger group discussion helped you gain further intercultural insights about improving relationships we have with those who are different from us?

12) What positive contributions can you make in your community/in your context?

Following this discussion/debriefing, there could be further discussion about next steps in developing intercultural competence, including any follow-up as well as expectations about maintaining the connections/relationships within the group.

This could be followed by some sort of performance, music recording, meaningful quote, or even a group photo or group goodbye.

Remember to discuss next steps, including completion of personal action plans for developing intercultural competencies as well as expectations on continuing contact, relationship building, and intercultural dialogue.

PARTICIPANT'S ACTION PLAN HANDOUT

Intercultural competence include the following elements: Respect, openness, flexibility, curiosity, cultural self-awareness, understanding others' perspectives, culture-specific knowledge, listening for understanding, observing, empathy, adaptability, communication skills

1. Identify 2-3 intercultural elements that you would like to focus on for yourself:

(example: become more culturally self-aware of my own cultural background and its impact on my behavior and communication, adapt my communication to others, think about others' perspectives on different issues, become a better listener/observer, listen more for understanding)

2. What will you do to further enhance, develop, and practice these intercultural elements?

(examples: build an authentic relationship with someone from a different background, learn more about another's culture, look for the invisible influence of culture in everything, meet regularly with someone from a different background, read a book on intercultural communication, take an intercultural course, learn a new language, attend a community event intended primarily for a group other than my own, actively reflect on my intercultural competence development, regularly seek out others different from me)

3. How will you continue to engage specifically in a positive manner with those who are different from you? What else will you do to further intercultural competencies?

STRATEGIES FOR BECOMING MORE INTERCULTURALLY COMPETENT

1) Seek first to understand – listen for understanding!
2) Value others as fellow humans
3) Recognize that the way you see the world is only one way – there are many other ways
4) Resist making assumptions about others
5) Assume positive intent (don't take it personally)
6) See culture's role in your own behavior, communication, and identity
7) Seek to understand culture's role in others' behavior, communication and identity
8) Learn more about how others communicate in face-to-face interactions (beyond words)
9) Adapt your communication to the expectations within the particular situation
10) Be intentional about engaging in positive intercultural interactions

---

Excerpted from *Manual for Developing Intercultural Competencies: Story Circles* by Darla K. Deardorff, UNESCO/Routledge 2020.

B. Criteria for facilitators of Story Circles

The role of facilitators in Story Circles is to introduce the process, provide instructions on the process (see the following), organize the participants into small groups, be available if any questions or issues arise while small groups are engaged in the Story Circle process, and facilitate the debrief of the experience. Note that it is important for facilitators to remain a part from the small groups and to NOT be a member of the small groups, since this impacts the power dynamic in the group.

Facilitator criteria include

- has a welcoming presence (meaning that they are approachable and calming);
- accepts everyone as worthy of respect and demonstrates respect appropriately;
- is comfortable in front of a group;
- is familiar with the context and backgrounds of the Story Circle participants (including awareness of cultural norms and expectations of the participants and of the culture in which the tool is being used);
- models *listening for understanding*, patience, and humility, and is willing to share authentically, meaning is comfortable with uncertainty and emotional exposure;
- is appropriate for the particular context (i.e., particular cultural contexts may suggest that those from a certain gender, religion, or age may be more appropriate as a facilitator based on the societal/social expectations within that particular context);
- can thoughtfully guide group discussion;
- ideally exhibits intercultural facilitation competencies (see the following); and
- relates well to those from different backgrounds (age, religion, socioeconomic status, culture, gender, and so on).

Intercultural facilitation competencies (excerpted from Bennett, 2012, p. 14)

The effective intercultural facilitator has the ability to

- communicate clearly to nonnative speakers of the language used in the program;
- facilitate multicultural groups (including taking turns, use of silence, etc.);
- adapt to different ways of communicating (verbally and nonverbally);
- suspend judgment of alternative cultural norms;
- recognize culture-specific risk factors for participants (loss of face, group identity, status, etc.);

- develop multiple frames of reference for interpreting behavior;
- demonstrate good judgment in selecting the most appropriate interpretation in an intercultural situation;
- ask sensitively phrased questions to avoid making assumptions or showing bias;
- avoid idioms, slang, colloquial language, and aphorisms;
- recognize bias in goals, content, process, materials, instructions;
- interpret nonverbal behavior in culturally appropriate ways;
- monitor the use of humor for cultural appropriateness; and
- display cultural humility through words and actions.

C. General tips for facilitators of Story Circles

The following are some general facilitation tips that came from the lessons learned through the five UNESCO pilots of the Story Circles methodology:

- Ensure that the marketing and invitation to Story Circles frame this as an experience and explicitly state the purpose (develop and practice intercultural competencies).
- Use co-facilitators when possible.
- Select and adapt the prompts to the specific context.
- Allow more time if possible (at least two hours).
- Be sure to allow enough time to debrief at the end.
- Divide into diverse groups of five when possible.
- Use a handout (see p. 71 for sample) if all participants are able to read the handout (do not assume literacy) so that groups can walk through the steps on their own.
- Be sure to emphasize the importance of practicing *listening for understanding* and explain what that means (see p. 27 in this manual).
- Be sure to emphasize the importance of maintaining confidentiality in the small groups.
- Note that the person who starts the personal story sharing in the small groups is the person whose birthday is "closest to today" (meaning either right before or soon after today's date) *and* that the person to the right makes note of the time for the storyteller (and indicates nonverbally using an agreed upon gesture when there is no more time).
- Facilitators need to make sure participants follow the instructions so that this does not devolve into a group discussion. The handout is helpful for this (if all participants are able to read it). If using the handout, it is helpful to highlight key elements before the groups begin and ensure that everyone commits to upholding the guidelines and holding each other accountable.
- Facilitators should not be part of the small groups and should not walk around to listen in on the small groups since this is a violation of confidentiality within the groups.
- Organizers may want to provide pre-reading materials on intercultural competencies, as well as participant profiles, if appropriate.
- Be sure to include an appropriate opening and ending to the experience (such as a quote or music), which can be designed/provided by the participants themselves.

D. Intercultural tips for Story Circle facilitators

- Communicate clearly by using simple language, paraphrasing, and rephrasing instructions.
- Refrain from asking yes/no questions.
- Refrain from calling on individuals specifically.
- Interpret communication and behavior (including nonverbal and what is *not* said) of participants in multiple ways.
- Be patient.
- Be very aware of how and what you are as the facilitator.
- Be very aware of the behaviors of your participants (observe and listen carefully) and try to understand those behaviors through the eyes of your participants, resisting judging them or interpreting such behaviors through your lens.
- Display cultural humility, meaning that you model a "willing and curious to learn" attitude that demonstrates that the facilitator's way of seeing the world is just one viewpoint (versus a "know-it-all" attitude of someone having "all the answers").

Additional intercultural training tips for facilitators

For those interested in engaging in further intercultural competencies development with participants beyond the use of Story Circles, and in utilizing additional intercultural tools, it is important to remember the following:

a) Develop clear and realistic goals around intercultural competencies development, remembering that participants are at different stages in their own intercultural development.
b) Meet participants where they are (find out what their needs and questions are) and ensure that the intercultural training (including content and activities) is relevant to participants (meaning that it meets their needs).
c) Create an appropriate and safe learning environment.
d) Match the training and learning activities with the stated training goals.
e) Recognize that a one-time intercultural training is usually insufficient for achieving the training goals (particularly regarding intercultural competencies development) and, ideally, needs to include several iterations of intercultural training over time.

(For more on designing and implementing intercultural competence training, see Gregersen-Hermans & Pusch, 2012).

E. Using Story Circles with children and youth

Story Circles works quite well with adults. When using Story Circles with children and youth (18 or younger), there are some adjustments that need to be made to the Story Circle process so that the experience can be more appropriate for the younger age group. Here are some tips to consider when using Story Circles with children and youth:

1) Do not use a handout (like the one found in Section III) but rather guide the group through the Story Circle process step-by-step as a whole group.
2) Ensure that there is enough time, including break time and creative reflective time.
3) Use a "talking piece" so that only one person talks at a time in the small groups when sharing their personal experiences (see p. 41).
4) Spend time reviewing the ground rules and use visuals to illustrate these ground rules.
5) Minimize distractions as much possible (even timekeeping devices can become a distraction although something like a sand timer may be useful as long as time element does not receive too much focus).
6) If in a school classroom, it may be helpful to have an outside facilitator instead of the teacher.
7) Debrief the Story Circles using only two or three questions and having the small groups create some sort of visual in response to each question (such as a collage).
8) If Story Circles are to be used in schools, it is crucial to have the support and "buy-in" from the school leadership.
9) If evaluations are used, it may be more useful to have pictures instead of wordy evaluation questions.

F. Creating a safe space

(Adapted from Chaitlin, 2003)

- Create a supportive environment (by following the instructions for implementing Story Circles in this manual).
- Ensure that all participants are voluntarily there (and that no coercion has occurred).
- Be very clear on the purpose of the Story Circles (to develop intercultural competencies).
- Model open, genuine, and honest communication from the very beginning of the Story Circle.
- Assure participants that within the group, all are considered equal (meaning that no one participant has more rights than others and that all are given equal respect) – equality within the circle is key in creating a safe space.
- Assure confidentiality – and get all to agree to only share with others' permission.
- Consider holding more than one meeting if it seems the group needs more time to get – acquainted, build trust, and feel comfortable with each other (see the challenges section of this manual for more on this).
- Establish and uphold ground rules together (some of which follow) – ground rules are key to establishing a safe space.

Some ground rules for Story Circles

1) Respect self and others.
2) Avoid making assumptions (although that's quite natural as humans to do).[1]
3) Don't take personal offense at what or how something is said.
4) Presume positive intent.
5) Speak only from personal experience and not on behalf of others.
6) Be genuine and authentic.
7) Refrain from judgmental or critical comments.
8) Maintain confidentiality.
9) Respond to others in your group as a fellow human.

Conditions for using Story Circles

*All participants are willing to be involved in the Story Circle process.
*Participants are interested in developing their intercultural competencies.
*Experienced facilitators are available to guide the Story Circle process.

*Provide a safe space (physically, mentally, emotionally) for this Story Circle process to occur.

*Provide sufficient time for the Story Circle process.

*Ensure the appropriateness for the societal and cultural expectations of the context.

*Affirm the adherence to confidentiality in what is shared.

*Affirm the equality of all participants in the circles.

Note

1 To avoid making assumptions, it is important to listen and observe very carefully first and then to consider different explanations for the communication issue at hand – this can often start by asking, "Help me understand why . . ." See additional tools for more on the OSEE tool.

G. General train-the-trainers outline*

Here's a general train-the-trainers outline for training Story Circles facilitators. The best way to train facilitators is to have them experience Story Circles.

Welcome, introductions, overview

Icebreaker activity

Defining intercultural competencies:

Activity: "Think of Someone Who..." (see Section III)

Discussion: Intercultural competencies Framework (see Figure 2.1 on page 59)

Introduction to Story Circles methodology

Review of manual contents

Get into small groups

Story Circles tool in small groups

Debrief as whole group

Reflection

Train-the-trainers Q&A

Action planning – when/where trained facilitators will use the Story Circles methodology

*Consider organizing a follow-up train-the-trainers session several weeks later

H. Defining intercultural competencies: "Think of someone who" activity

This activity can be done in both the train-the-trainers as well as in the Story Circles experience. This would be done toward the beginning to help focus participants on the purpose of Story Circles, which is to develop and practice intercultural competencies. This activity has been used in the initial UNESCO pilots and worked very well in helping to focus participants before introducing them to the Story Circles methodology.

> **Supplies needed:** "Stickie notes" (at least three per person), pens/pencils, and blank paper (one per every three people)
> **Time needed for the activity:** At least 30 minutes

Instructions

Provide a brief overview of the activity. Distribute three "stickie notes" per person. Ask everyone to "think of someone you know personally or who is known to you whom you feel does a really good job of connecting with others who are different from them – this could be differences related to gender, age, religion, ethnicity, geographic location, socio-economic background, and so on. You don't need to tell us who you are thinking of. However, on the stickie notes, you need to write a word or phrase – one word or phrase per paper – that describes this person and what it is about the person that makes him or her so successful in connecting with others."

Give participants time to write these words and phrases (and it can be more than three). Once everyone has written down some words and phrases, then put participants into groups of three and have them compare what they have written. As they do this, walk around and give each group a blank sheet of paper and ask the participants to post their stickie note papers on the blank paper and see what commonalities they have in their responses and any common themes that may emerge. They can group these together. If they have many different responses, that is acceptable too.

Once groups have discussed their responses and grouped them together, then have each group report out to the whole group on the results. The facilitator can write up the general themes. The facilitator then debriefs this activity with the whole group by asking questions such as the following: What common themes emerged? What surprised you? What does this say about what is necessary to get along together in spite of our differences?

At the end of this activity, the facilitator can highlight the responses that are related to the goals of the Story Circles experience and say that the groups have just described intercultural competencies. Then, if appropriate, distribute the intercultural competencies framework (Figure 2.1 on page 59) and highlight some key points from this framework.

I. Frequently asked questions

What is unique about this methodology? Story Circles are a structured yet adaptable tool that allows participants to actually practice intercultural competencies and allows for emotional connections that may not occur through more traditional intercultural training. Because of participants' emotional connection, this methodology tends to be more transformative than traditional training.

What is the difference between Story Circles and storytelling? Story Circles are a thoughtful process that involves a group of people sharing personal experiences in a circle often for purposes of mediation, restorative justice, and, in the case of the UNESCO methodology, for developing intercultural competencies. Storytelling is a cultural and social activity usually involving a broader audience for the purposes of entertainment, education, moral formation, or cultural preservation.

Who can be a facilitator of Story Circles? Facilitators of Story Circles should be experienced teachers or trainers, who relate well to people from many different kinds of backgrounds. Facilitators should be able to model some of the targeted intercultural competencies, such as *listening for understanding* and be knowledgeable about and appropriate for the context of the Story Circles. (Facilitator criteria can be found on p. 79.)

How many participants are in a small group, and what's the minimum and maximum number of participants? Ideally, five in a small group, no fewer than four and no more than six. There's really no maximum number of participants as long as the space can accommodate the number and the facilitators are able to organize the participants into diverse groups of five. The minimum number would be around eight to ten, so there can be two small groups.

What ages is this for? Story Circles has been successfully piloted with participants ages 12–70+, so it is designed to work with a wide range of ages.

How long does it take to run Story Circles? Story Circles usually take a minimum of 90 minutes, although 120 minutes is preferred so that there is enough time to debrief the experience (and more time if Story Circles are a part of a larger event).

Can we skip the debriefing/discussion time at the end? The debriefing/discussion time as a whole group at the end is a very important part of the methodology and involves reflection time as well as discussion on lessons learned during the experience and next steps on continuing to develop one's intercultural competencies. It is crucial to allow sufficient time for this debriefing phase. This debriefing time can include small groups sharing back with the larger group, possibly through a visual presentation (poster) or a song, dance, or poetry (see p. 37 for other suggestions on the debrief).

Why are there strict time parameters to the sharing of personal stories? Time parameters are established so that everyone is ensured of having equal time in the group and that no one person dominates. It is important that the small group agree on a nonverbal sign to show that time is finished and that each person commits to adhering to the time limitations. It is also important to rotate the timekeeper role so that one person is not viewed as controlling the time. It is also important not to fixate on the time but instead continue practicing *listening for understanding.*

Can there be mandatory participation? Ideally no – participation should not be mandatory since this really needs to involve willing participants who understand the purpose of the Story Circles experience as developing intercultural competencies and who are interested and motivated to participate because of that purpose.

Can there be observers? Ideally, it's best not to have observers since observers will not be part of the small groups and cannot listen in due to the confidentiality of what is shared in each small group.

What if there is not much diversity in the group? Depending on the context, the group can decide the diversity criteria for dividing into small groups. Or facilitators can assign members to small groups based on gender, generation, religion, urban/rural factors, or any other relevant factors that would ensure that small groups have a diversity of perspectives.

Can participants take notes to help remember the flashbacks? If participants do not think they can remember the memorable part of each story for the others in their group, they can briefly make a note. However, participants should not engage in full note taking since that could be seen as not fully *listening for understanding* as well as a violation of confidentiality.

What does "*listening for understanding*" mean? It means focusing 100% on the speaker – to what is being said, how it is said, nonverbals that may be present, to what is not said. It is *not* interrupting, asking questions, making comments, and so on since that would mean the focus is more on the listener.

Why can not we just have a discussion? Why do we have to follow this process? A discussion involves a very different process from a circle process and will not achieve the same goals for developing intercultural competencies. It is very important to follow the process as outlined in this manual for the intercultural goals to be achieved. Further, this process has been successfully piloted in all five UNESCO regions around the world and the Story Circle process works well in achieving the stated goals around intercultural competencies.

Is this just a one-time experience, or can it be repeated? If the same group of participants will be together again, then this Story Circles experience can be repeated again (in fact, in some school classes, teachers use this once a week with different prompts).

Can someone "pass" in a small group and not share a personal story? Someone could "pass" initially, but everyone needs to share a personal story, even if someone shares a more surface-level story – this is about mutual sharing of all participants.

What if someone does not want to be vulnerable enough to share? Participants can decide the degree to which they are vulnerable by choosing the depth to which they wish to share their own experiences. For example, the personal experience they choose to share can be a more meaningful one or a more surface-level experience, the latter of which would not require as much vulnerability.

What if someone seems to dominate or lead in the small group? The structured nature of this process should help curtail the tendency for someone to dominate the small group. It is important for all group members to commit initially to upholding the guidelines and holding each other accountable in a respectful manner. If there is concern about someone dominating the group, a talking piece becomes very useful, which means only the person who is holding the talking piece can speak.

Is there potential for (emotional) harm? While there is always potential for deeper sharing that could be quite emotional, it is important for facilitators to choose appropriate prompts that will elicit the level of sharing desired. It is also important for group members to commit to respecting each other and upholding the guidelines. If there is concern that someone may not share as appropriately as needed in the small group, then there may need to be a trained facilitator (also called a "circle keeper") in each group (this could also possibly be done as a larger facilitated group if there are concerns regarding the degree of sharing). See p. 41 for more on challenges.

Do Story Circles develop intercultural competencies? Intercultural competencies are a lifelong process so participating in this experience is one step in that journey. Story Circles provide an opportunity for participants to practice some key intercultural skills (such as *listening for understanding*) and hone some aspects of intercultural competencies.

How can the outcomes be assessed from the Story Circles experience? Depending on the context, an evaluation form may be distributed (see p. 93) at the end of the experience, and if possible, there can be a follow-up with participants six to eight weeks out from the experience. In either case, the emphasis should be on what changes they will make in their interactions with others who are different from them. There can also be follow-up on action plans, if completed. Guided reflection can also be a way of gauging the impact, including through group "presentations" to the whole group on what they learned (this can be presented visually as a poster, through a poem, etc.). In assessing outcomes, it is important to have clearly stated outcomes in the beginning of the experience and then collect evidence that those outcomes were met by participants.

What are the next steps after a Story Circles experience? Ideally, there would be time to have participants develop an action plan (see Figure 2.1 on p. 59), and pending the context, it would be recommended to have follow-up sessions if possible, so this goes beyond a one-time experience (see p. 44).

How can participants use the skills they practice in Story Circles? Participants will hopefully be able to immediately use some of the skills they practiced in Story Circles in their daily lives – for example, by committing to take more time to listen and to using *listening for understanding* in their conversations and interactions with others in their daily lives since such deep listening is an important tool in bridging divides. Following a Story Circles experience, participants will be more open-minded when connecting to others, to be more aware of their own stereotypes and biases, to be curious about different perspectives, and to be slower to form snap judgments about others; they will take time to more intentionally develop intercultural competencies in themselves every day; they will see that everyone they encounter each day has a story to share and that there are many ways we are similar to others, even when it seems like there are so many differences that divide us.

Why should the facilitators *not* be part of the circle or listen in on the circles? Facilitators for Story Circles should not be part of a circle (unlike typical circle processes that have "circle keepers") since they would be viewed as having "more power" in the circle; it is important that the participants view each other as equal in the circle. Facilitators should also not "listen in" on the circles given the importance of maintaining confidentiality within the group.

What happens if someone comes late after the Story Circles have started? Given the importance of establishing trust within the group, it is very difficult for anyone to join a Story Circle after the rounds have already started. Facilitators will need to be creative in integrating latecomers in an appropriate manner so as not to disrupt the group or the trust already established among the other members; otherwise, it may be best to brief latecomers on what is happening but not have them participate in the Story Circles.

What about the use of nonverbal communication when listening to others' experiences? While it is not possible to interrupt, comment, or ask questions during or following each person's personal sharing, *appropriate*, *respectful* nonverbal responses are possible. Facilitators may want to note this during the instruction time and emphasize the importance of ensuring that nonverbal responses are appropriate within the context and that participants should monitor their own nonverbal responses to ensure *appropriateness and respect*.

Can we take a break between the end of the Story Circles and the debriefing time? No, it is best to conduct the debriefing discussion time immediately following the Story Circles while the experience itself is still "fresh" for participants.

Can the Story Circles process be adapted (such as adjusting the time requirements)? Yes, the process presented in the Manual is meant to give a clear idea of how the Story Circles process works for developing intercultural competence and this process can and should be adapted to the participants and to each specific context, as long as adaptations are grounded in the guidelines (such as all participants get the equal amount of time and so on) outlined in this Manual.

What if power/status levels are perceived to be a barrier for participants? If power/status differentiations (for example, professors and students in the same circle) may be a barrier to authentic participation in the Story Circles, it may be better to create circles of similar groups (for example, groups of students and groups of professors).

What if participants see this more as a performance? It is important to emphasize in the beginning that this is about sharing from participants' own perspective/experience in an authentic manner and not about engaging in storytelling as a performance. See the first question here about the difference between Story Circles and Storytelling.

What are the best ways to conclude the Story Circles experience with participants? Debriefing the Story Circles experience with the whole group is very important and in addition to the debriefing questions provided in this manual (p. 76) there are a number of suggested ways to conclude the Story Circles experience (found on p. 37) including individuals engaging in action planning (see action planning handout on p. 78), having each group present their main lessons learned/insights from the experience (including in creative ways such as a poster presentation or song), providing a summary of the experience and emphasizing again the purpose and goals, concluding with an appropriate quote or song that is familiar to participants.

J. UNESCO evaluation form

STORY CIRCLES FEEDBACK QUESTIONNAIRE

Please take a few moments to comment on the activity you have just completed. Your feedback is valuable, as it will help us know how best to improve the delivery of the activity in the future.

Confidentiality Statement

All responses will be kept strictly confidential. No links will be provided to individual responses in the event that names are provided. Data will only be used for internal evaluation.

Activity details

Facilitator	Venue	Date of Activity

Activity feedback

Instructions: Tick the appropriate response below and add any comments you have about the program.

---

1. The activity helped me respect other people more.

   Not at all ☐ ☐ ☐ ☐ ☐ Fully

---

2. The activity helped me understand the skill "listen for understanding." I can listen to other participants' views and experiences to understand their situations and beliefs.

   Not at all ☐ ☐ ☐ ☐ ☐ Fully

---

3. The activity made me want to find out about the similarities and differences of people from different backgrounds.

   Not at all ☐ ☐ ☐ ☐ ☐ Fully

---

4. The activity helped me to understand how I view the world.

   Not at all ☐ ☐ ☐ ☐ ☐ Fully

5. The activity helped me to understand what other people are thinking or feeling.

   Not at all ☐   ☐   ☐   ☐   ☐ Fully

6. The activity helped me understand how my own values, beliefs, and actions can affect others experiences.

   Not at all ☐   ☐   ☐   ☐   ☐ Fully

7. The activity helped me build relationships with people from different backgrounds.

   Not at all ☐   ☐   ☐   ☐   ☐ Fully

8. The length of the activity was appropriate.

   Not at all ☐   ☐   ☐   ☐   ☐ Fully

9. The activity was well planned and organized.

   Not at all ☐   ☐   ☐   ☐   ☐ Fully

10. The activity was a good investment of my time.

    Not at all ☐   ☐   ☐   ☐   ☐ Fully

11. I intend to use the skills and knowledge acquired in this activity.

    Not at all ☐   ☐   ☐   ☐   ☐ Fully

Comments: _____

_____

_____

_____

12. Write down three (3) actions you will now do as a result of this activity.

    1. _____

       _____

2. _____

_____

3. _____

_____

13. I would recommend this activity to others.

Not at all ☐   ☐   ☐   ☐ Fully

Facilitator

Instructions: Tick the appropriate response below and add any comments you have about the program.

14. The facilitator had a thorough understanding of the activity.

Not at all ☐   ☐   ☐   ☐ Fully

15. The facilitator was effective in meeting the activity's objectives.

Not at all ☐   ☐   ☐   ☐ Fully

16. I would recommend this facilitator for other activities.

Not at all ☐   ☐   ☐   ☐ Fully

Comments: _____

_____

_____

Overall

17. How would you improve this activity?

_____

_____

18.   What are the strengths of this activity?

_____

_____

19. What are the weaknesses of this activity?

_____

_____

Any further comments

Comments:

_____

_____

_____

Personal information – optional

Name	Organization	Gender	Age

Country	Email		

Additional questions

Instructions: Tick the appropriate response below and answer the questions.

20. This activity met my expectation.

Not at all ☐   ☐   ☐   ☐ Fully

21. I would like more follow-up sessions.

Not at all ☐   ☐   ☐   ☐ Fully

22. What did you find challenging?

_____

_____

23. What was your motivation to attend the session?

_____

_____

_____

24. What aspects could have been longer or shorter?

_____

_____

_____

25. Where will you use the skills you have learned?

_____

_____

Thank you!

Index

Note: numbers in italics indicate figures and numbers in bold indicate tables on the corresponding pages.

Printed in the United States
by Baker & Taylor Publisher Services